Wealth from Within
The Real "Secret" to Using the Law of Attraction

By Lori Culwell

Legal Notice

The Publisher has strived to be as accurate and complete as possible in the creation of this report, notwithstanding the fact that he does not warrant or represent at any time that the contents within are accurate due to the rapidly changing nature of the Internet.

While all attempts have been made to verify information provided in this publication, the Publisher assumes no responsibility for errors, omissions, or contrary interpretation of the subject matter herein. Any perceived slights of specific persons, peoples, or organizations are unintentional.

In practical advice books, like anything else in life, there are no guarantees of income made. Readers are cautioned to reply on their own judgment about their individual circumstances to act accordingly.

This book is not intended for use as a source of legal, business, accounting or financial advice. All readers are advised to seek services of competent professionals in legal, business, accounting, and finance field.

Table of Contents

Free Bonuses

Hey look—you're attracting prosperity already!

Visit this link:

http://wealthfromwithinbook.com/resources

to get the following books for free:

1. *Think and Grow Rich*, by Napoleon Hill

2. *The Master Key System*, by Charles Haanel

3. *Thoughts are Things*, by Prentice Mulford

4. *Our Invisible Supply: How to Obtain*, by Frances Larimer Warner

5. *The Science of Getting Rich*, by Wallace Wattles

6. *Your Invisible Power*, by Genevieve Behrend

Plus, a special audio bonus you can use for meditation!

Introduction:
An Energetic Epiphany

2003 was by far the worst year of my life, and yet, the lessons I've learned since then have made me the person I am today. That year, I had what Eckhart Tolle would call an "awakening." Like many others who've had life-changing experiences, it started with a dramatic turn of events. In one week, I turned thirty, was burned in the face in an accident, and my mother (who was 59 at the time) suddenly died from an aneurysm. It was, by far, the most traumatic and stressful time of my life, so I guess it makes sense that I threw myself into "personal development" type books to give that time period some meaning.

I've always been an "I want to know everything there is to know about a subject" kind of person, so I moved quickly through all of the personal development literature and programs I could find. Before my mother's death, I guess I figured I had all the time in the world, but now it seemed like the opposite—it was like I was suddenly more aware of how short life can be, and I wanted to get the most out of mine. I could not waste a single moment. I wanted more from my life, and I wanted it now. At the same time, I was sure that the pessimistic attitude I'd been so fond of before wasn't helping me one bit. By 2005, when I was lucky enough to be one of the first people to view a still-underground version of a movie called "The Secret," I had already been using the tools of creative visualization and goal-setting to make major achievements in my life. I had begun investing in real estate, and now own properties in Texas, California, Florida, and Costa Rica. I'd started a consulting business, and it was quickly becoming successful.   I self-published a book, and it sold so many copies, it was picked up and re-released by Simon & Schuster. Outwardly I was successful and had achieved many of the goals I set out for myself.   I was making things happen!

And yet, despite all of these "wins," I still felt there was something missing to the whole "law of attraction" thing, since it seemed to be so hit or miss. I never felt like I was in "the flow" that people talked about, I usually felt like I was forcing things, and I really didn't have "faith" in the traditional sense that if I just "released my goals into the universe," they would magically materialize. Yet, this is exactly what seemed to be happening to some of my friends, one of whom set the intention to adopt a baby and six months later, through a series of coincidences I won't even try to describe, was mother to baby born right down the street from her house. This was all very interesting to me.

Why, I wondered, did some of my goals seem to materialize, but others went absolutely nowhere? Why were some of my friends using the law of attraction to make huge gains in their lives, while others applied this law and saw no difference at all?

This seemed like an interesting mystery to me, and so I set out to try to quantify just what it was that separated hugely successful people (like Oprah-successful) from mere high achievers. In as scientific a way as possible, I read back over all the books and interviewed people who had successfully (and unsuccessfully) used the "law of attraction," and yet, I still couldn't figure it out. Why did some people's lives come together and some didn't? There had to be a logical explanation, even in the invisible realm of thought (and other things unseen).

I wish I could say the answer came to me right away, but it didn't. Actually, it wasn't until mid-2008, when I looked at my list of goals for the year, that I had an epiphany. While looking at one of the goals, my first thought was "oh, I have to do some visualization on that," then my very next thought was "ugh—I don't have any more energy for visualization."

I don't have any more energy for visualization.

Hmmm...

I don't know why, but this statement was so interesting to me that I mulled it over for three or four days, then went back to all my notes and research. What if *energy supply* was the missing component behind the successful visualizations? After all, Rhonda Byrne did briefly mention (in The Secret) that all of the spiritual teachers in the movie practiced meditation, and it seemed people who meditated and kept themselves in a state of gratitude, joy, and other happy emotions were able to manifest things more quickly and easily. So—what if it was just a "supply and demand" issue? Maybe my "supply" of energy had been depleted or somehow wasn't reaching my goals. That made sense—if I could just build up more energy and direct it through visualization; I figured things would start working better.

I know, this conclusion seems surprisingly simple, but it turned out to be right. It took awhile, but when I finally found a meditation practice that worked for me and really tried to put myself in gratitude and joy more often, things started to work better and didn't seem as hard. I started having those "think of someone and then they call you" moments all the time, I got money in the mail unexpectedly, and I totally lost that sense of "I have to make something happen right now" that had been making me nuts. Energy, as it turns out, was the thing I was missing, and once I got in the habit of regularly building it up (which I am still doing), things fell back into place. It felt like I finally figured out the secret *behind* "The Secret."

One Step Further: I Apply My Epiphany to the Economy

So, what if this is true for everyone else who's been using the law of attraction since it became part of the collective consciousness a few years ago? We can probably all agree that we've just experienced one of the hardest economic periods in our history. Starting in 2007 with a revelation about mortgage-backed securities, it soon became clear that we were in for an economic roller-coaster ride that has reached as far and wide as any in our history. Unemployment rose, housing prices tanked, and there was bad news seemingly around every corner.

But why? How could we have fallen so far from the heights of only a few years before? Weren't we all feeling prosperous and abundant? Didn't we all read (or see) "The Secret?" Don't we know that "thoughts become things?" Did we all just suddenly start thinking "bad thoughts?" What about "unlimited abundance for everyone" and "ask and ye shall receive?" What about visualization and the law of attraction? Did we (without knowing it) attract a recession? Certainly no one would consciously attract or align themselves with the kind of hard times we were seeing all around us.

When I applied my own "energetic epiphany" to this situation, it seemed like we've been overzealously using the law of attraction, writing "visualization" checks that our supplies of energy just couldn't keep up with, and we then swung into a sort of "energy deficit" that was reflected as a recession.

Is it possible that if we all started building up our own energy supplies again, we could turn things around more quickly than the natural ebb and flow of the economy over time?

I believe that the answer is yes. We are on the brink of a completely new understanding of how energy works, and this solution starts from within each one of us. What is needed is not just to visualize, but to connect and tap into our own sources of energy in order to replenish the supply and correct the imbalance. We are currently tapped out, but with a simple shift in consciousness, we can put ourselves back on track.

What if visualization isn't what you think it is? What if, instead of **attracting** what you desired, your goals were actually being **created** from your own supply of energy? That is to say, what if you've used up all the energy **behind** what you were visualizing, and that's why your fortune has started to dry up?

The good news is, since you have the ability to tap into (and start rebuilding) your supply of energy at any time, you are essentially your own bank, and you can use meditation and pleasurable activities as your own economic stimulus package.

Lingo, Hippies, and People Who Give You a Weird Vibe

Some experts and gurus in this field use language that, frankly, is off-putting to regular people. Personally, New Age music makes my skin crawl, and the minute I hear someone using the word "chakra," I start to think "this person is not going to be able to help me, they do not live in the real world where I live." I mean, I don't care if people say they channel spirits, but what I really want to know is: what do those spirits have to tell me that will be relevant to my life here on Earth? I acknowledge that I am a spiritual being having a physical experience, but my mission is to meld those two things as much as possible so that my physical experience is what I want it to be, and to help you do so as well.

Unfortunately, the subject itself (energy) lends itself to people who slip into double-talk with phrases like "resonating with the vibrational tonality of your feelings," or "really feeling your way into the realness of who you are," both of which sound so hippie (to me) they make it hard to take the concepts seriously. Maybe the people who say these things don't eat enough meat to be grounded. Maybe what they are saying makes sense to them. All I know is that I was searching for a "common sense" approach to these concepts, and since I couldn't find what I was looking for, I created one.

Of course, that's not to say that these terms don't work for some people. Anything that has meaning for you and helps you get in touch with your own energy is fine. If you find yourself rolling your eyes at the terms people use, just take the overall message and disregard what doesn't speak to you, or find a different teacher.

So, just for our purposes here, let's agree—no new phrases or terms. No "vibrational tonality." No "realness of who you are." No chakra clearing. For now, let's agree that everything is made of energy, and that by becoming aware of our *own* energy, we create more favorable circumstances in our lives. We can do these things without losing our edge, turning all woo-woo, or writing songs that are completely lacking in irony. How we do this is up to us—whether it's by listening to music you like, or helping out a friend in need, or taking some deep breaths on a regular basis, or really feeling grateful for things that are going well. We don't need clever expressions, or angels on our shoulders, or remote viewing capabilities (not yet, anyway). We need to know ourselves, and to feel our own aliveness. Call it whatever you want.

No, really. Call it whatever makes you feel comfortable, because I guarantee, you are not getting any closer to your goals when you're rolling your eyes at someone else's fake enthusiasm. Take what you need from spiritual teachers, and let the rest go. Not connecting with someone's personality or choice of music or "bag of energy tricks" is not going to hold you back any longer. My intention with this book is to provide as clear and "common sense" a method for understanding these things as possible, so that we can all be on the same page, and so no one is left behind just because they don't understand the language of one teacher.

Besides, who is to say that the topic of an unseen, immeasurable "bank account" of energy won't be a common topic of conversation in ten years? Twenty? Now more than ever, we possess not only the intellectual capacity to understand a higher consciousness, but also the capacity to expand that consciousness to build our storehouses of energy and change our lives like never before. Now is the time to make the connection between the "energy of the universe," your own feeling of "aliveness" and how this energy is realized in your life.

This book, then, is really a compilation of my conclusions, and how I have put these conclusions into practice in my everyday life. I've waded through some nonsense, talked to a lot of people, and have tried all of this myself, so I'm glad to be able to share some stuff that's worked for me. We'll mainly be talking about energy: your energy. We'll also cover coincidences, and money, and making things in your life run more smoothly. I'm assuming that you're reading this book because, like many people, you sensed that there was a missing piece to all that talk about the law of attraction, and you wanted to take it further. But, just like anything—if something sounds ridiculous to you or like it just wouldn't work for you, don't do it! The challenge here is for you to find out what connects you to your own life energy, so you can be more connected and allow things to go better in your life. Take from it what works, and feel free to leave the rest behind. This information is out there—it's just a matter of forming a larger understanding of what is relevant to you so that you can build your own energy supply and get your life the way you want it. So, really, this is all about you. My sincere hope is that something in this book makes you go "Wow, that makes sense," and from there you will start the path that leads to higher consciousness and a whole new life.

Believe me, if I can do it, so can you.

1

Energy: A New Understanding of Where Things Really Come From

We are on the brink of a completely new understanding of how the world works.

Lynn McTaggart, author of "The Field" and "The Intention Experiment."

What We Know

Let's start with something about which we can all agree, regardless of our personal, spiritual, or religious beliefs.

Everyone knows the difference between "alive" and "dead," right? We can all agree that there is an animating force or "energy" to people who are alive. This energy can be gone in the very next minute, once someone has passed away.

What *is* this energy, exactly? Some would say the person's "soul" has left, or they might offer a more religious explanation of where that soul might have gone, but we can probably all agree that the energy that was there, which was beating their heart and keeping their bodily systems running, is now gone.

To take this one step further, can you feel that energy in yourself? Right now, if you stop everything, close your eyes, and try to clear your mind of your to-do list and random thoughts, can you feel that steady hum of life energy in the background? Better yet, close your eyes and try to "feel" the inside of your body, right under the surface. First your fingers, then your toes, then everything in between. Can you feel the energy of life in there somewhere? Or, if you can't feel it (yet), consider this: what does it feel like when you see or hear something very stirring, like a beautiful piece of art or literature, or a breathtaking sunset? Do you get chills? Goosebumps?

Did you feel it, or at least remember how it felt? Maybe you never thought about it before, or you were taking for granted the fact that it was there. Maybe it was never something you thought you could notice, but now you realize you can.

Now, another question: when do you feel the **most** alive? That is to say, when is this "energy" the strongest? Is it when you're surfing, or playing with your kids, or listening to Yo-Yo Ma play Bach's cello suites? Is it while performing stand-up comedy, or meditating, or scrapbooking with friends?

This feeling, the awareness of your own life energy, is where we will start. Isn't it what we all live for anyway, because it makes us feel so good when we're connected to it? Don't we consider ourselves "in the flow" if we can keep that feeling for a prolonged period of time, like when you're doing something and you look up at the clock to find that three hours have passed?

Now that you're thinking about what makes you feel "alive," let's go even a little deeper into that energy itself. We can probably all agree by now that "everything is made from energy," as has been mentioned in many studies of the law of attraction, quantum physics, and spirituality.

And, if everything is made from energy, and you've just (in the previous paragraph) identified that you can feel energy inside yourself, doesn't it then figure that you should be able to tap into this energy, to get "in the flow" so that you feel it all the time?

What if you could take that very same energy (or aliveness) and direct it to create the reality you want? We're literally talking "energy into matter" here, what some people would call "alchemy."

Also, what if you're already been doing this without even knowing it?

The thing is, if you've been visualizing or have gotten into the law of attraction or "The Secret" at all, you're already tapping into your supply of energy. It's been forming what you've been visualizing. You've already been doing the "into matter" part. What you might be missing is a connection to that energy component, so at this point you might be running a little low on supply.

OK, that was a lot to take in, all at once like that. It took me three years to research and write this book, so if you want to take a break and go get a glass of water, that's fine.

The Time is Now: Energy in Everyday Consciousness

This level of comprehension and ease with the subject of energy has been a long (long) time in coming. So, why are we talking about this now?

At this point in our human evolution and comprehension of consciousness, we have actually all agreed that everything is made of energy, and we have just now expanded our thinking enough for this to include things we can't see, like electricity, and atoms, and thoughts. Practically every day, we are confronted with new examples of this, whether it's Masaru Emoto's amazing water experiments, or stories of energy-based healing, or the recent discovery of the Higgs boson particle (better known as the "God particle"). Clearly, there is more to the world than what we can see and comprehend, and we are in the process of coming to an entirely new understanding of what these unseen things mean to us in our lives.

The popularity of "The Secret" is proof that we are on the brink of a complete shift in our understanding of how energy works. It just so happened that the first step was understanding how to direct it with our thoughts. Now, on to the next level—the energy that is backing up those visualizations and creating your life. To get right to it—the power to create your dreams and desires is literally **within** you. That "aliveness" you were feeling before, when you paid attention to it?

It's energy—and by putting your awareness on it, you are building it up, then directing it into what you want. **You** are energy, what you **want** is energy—you are the cosmic go-between, the "sorcerer" whose job it is to direct it. The source of that energy, at least for you, is your awareness of your own life force.

Sounds simple, right? So why didn't this breakthrough in metaphysical thinking happen before now? Why isn't this concept just common knowledge already?

Here it is, in terms as plain as they can be, given that we're talking about something that can't yet be seen or measured, but that we all agree is a force that is real and at work in the universe. It's about energy—*your* energy, to be exact.

1. Everything is made of energy.

2. You are made of energy.

3. When you develop an awareness of your *own* energy, or "life force" (through meditation, doing things that bring you joy, and staying in the present moment), you build up more of it.

4. This "energy" is yours to direct. You just need to make it into material things and experiences using visualization and other tools. The law of attraction, then, is really a law of creation, applying only to your own energy, which you are using to create your life and experiences. In short, thoughts become things, but only if you have the energy to back them up. Simple supply and demand.

Considering all of this, what do you think about your own energy supply? Do you have enough for all of your desires and everything you're visualizing? If you're not tapped in to your supply, then chances are you don't have enough, at least at the moment.

But, where did it start to go wrong? If you started working with the tools in "The Secret" or Shakti Gawain's "Creative Visualization," set some goals, did some visualization, and noticed some "coincidences," you definitely had some energy to spare. If you actually got some of the things on your list (like a new car, new job, or a new relationship), you probably had a decent amount.

However, after awhile, you might have noticed that things were getting more difficult or like you were having to force them. That meant your energy supply was running low. Your gas tank of this energy was flashing the yellow symbol, meaning you needed to pull over and fill up. But, you didn't know about the energy connection then, so you did what any motivated, ambitious person would do. You redoubled your efforts, going about your work, your visualization, and your positive attitude with even more determination. You were going to turn the situation around, just through sheer force of will. You might have even become a little bit manic.

But again, nothing happened. And then the creeping sense of doubt reared its ugly head. What happened to "thoughts become things?" shouted your thinking mind. "Has this whole thing been for nothing? Where's my stuff?" "When are things going to turn around??"

If you then started wondering about what you did wrong, trying even harder to get into vibrational harmony (or wondering what that meant), then obsessing about what you didn't have and wondering why no one would call you back and why you couldn't get anything done, that was the point where your energy supply had reached the zero balance. The car was out of gas, so to speak. You were stuck. You knew it, everyone around you knew it, and you couldn't think of a single other thing you could do to help yourself.

At that point, you probably gave up and said "who cares? Nothing's working out anyway, so I'm going to go walk on the beach, or go to a movie, or see my funny friend who cheers me up." Since you'd tried and tried and failed to achieve the goal, you stopped focusing on it and did something that made you feel good instead, maybe because you just couldn't take any more bad news. Then...mysteriously, things started to work out again. You got money in the mail unexpectedly, or a job came through, or your health improved for no reason. You were back in the flow!

But, why? Ever wonder why it is that once we take our attention off of the goal and "give up," things start to fall into place?

Again, it's because of energy. By visualizing and focusing on the goal without having a connection to the source of the supply, you were writing bad checks. When you gave up and went out to have a good time, you got back into the flow, and your energy was freed up to move in the direction of the goal. What you were doing by trying to cheer yourself up was, in effect, the same thing as going to an energy gas station. Meditation does the same thing, as does listening to music, spending time with animals, or whatever brings out that feeling of aliveness in you. What works best for you?

Now is absolutely the right time for you to move your attention from visualization and goal-setting over to building the energy that your goals are literally made of - that energy that you're going to tap into right now, to get your life "in the flow."

2

Your Energy: Quantity and Supply

As you're considering some new truths about energy and where your stuff is actually coming from, let's talk about peoples' energy supplies in action, so you'll maybe stop comparing yourself to other people once and for all. To be specific: why do some people have so much more in their lives than others, and how can we expand our own "flow" of energy so that we can have the lives we are visualizing?

Every one of us is born with a certain amount of energy (supply), though it is not yet possible to measure or quantify. You, right now, have enough energy to keep you alive (though for an unknown amount of time), and probably to get you some things and life circumstances that you desire. In other cultures, this energy has also been called **chi** or **prana**. Others call it "life essence," or "spirit of God." You can call it whatever you like, as long as you start developing an awareness of it, and through that awareness start increasing your supply as soon as possible.

If all of this sounds unbelievable, just take a look around you. Why is it that some people's lives seem "charmed," like they start talking about something and then everything falls into place for them? Why does "The Secret" work so much better for some people than for others? If the law of attraction is truly a law, shouldn't it work universally, like the laws of gravity or motion?

To form a better understanding of how each of us has a different quantity of energy at our disposal, let's talk about it in terms of something more mainstream (and yet still just as mysterious): your metabolism. A woman I know has always been lucky in that she can eat whatever she wants and still weighs 110 pounds. Even after having two babies and eating countless peanut butter M and M's, there is not an ounce of fat on her. Why? She eats the same amount (or more) as a grown man, yet stays the same tiny size.

Before you go directly to, "Who cares? I hate that person!" consider that the difference in her weight has almost solely do to with something that was, up until a few years ago, impossible to measure— her metabolism. And, while scientists and personal trainers are now able to calculate your metabolic rate, they'll also tell you that everyone's rate is different, and that there's no rhyme or reason as to why. That woman can eat whatever she wants and doesn't have to exercise, because her metabolism is just fast. Another person (maybe you!) can watch their calories like a hawk and get daily exercise, and still gain weight at the very mention of the word "cupcake."

You might be wondering, what's the point of all this (possibly depressing) metabolic talk? Well, it is helpful if you think of your energy supply in the same way. Everyone's metabolism is different, just as everyone's supply of energy is different, and some have better access to their "flow" than others, either because of beliefs that they've grown up with, or experiences that they've had, or for some other unknown reason. Every one of us is unique, and every one of us is challenged with finding our own connection with our "aliveness" or energy, just as each one of us has to figure out our own metabolism and act accordingly. Nothing to take personally or feel "slighted" about— just like some of us have to go to the gym every day in order to eat chocolate cake, some of us are going to have to put a little effort into connecting and building up this energy so that our dreams will come true.

But, just to be totally clear—this is not about "hard work," as you've known it before. If you've got an "average" amount of energy (that is, if you're not Oprah), you can put in as many sixteen hour days as you want, and you're probably still not going to have that breakthrough success you've been visualizing, because the energy just isn't there to back it up. In order to make that "quantum leap" into the realm of the truly connected and successful, you don't just need to change your thinking (though that helps as well)-- you need to develop a new habit of connecting to and building up your own energy supply. Only you know what it feels like when you're "connected" to your energy, so the answer is going to be different for everyone.

To clarify, then—if you're not living the life you want right now, even after multiple years of visualization, goal setting, and hard work, *you're not doing anything wrong.* You're just missing a step—your connection to your energy.

The fact is, you could be an absolute master of visualization, or declarations, or vibrational harmony with the goal (whatever that means) and still never get there, simply because you lack the *supply of energy* to back these intentions up.

The only problem you could possibly have, then, is one you could easily solve by connecting to your higher self, your own life energy. And in fact, when people awaken to their own consciousness, when they discover Eckhart Tolle's work and start to become more "present," or start meditating or going to yoga (or doing something else that by accident connects them with their energy), they find that things start to turn around. What they don't know is why, which is what we're talking about here. Because being aware of your energy is not just something you do because you're trying to be a nicer person or "live more in the moment."

Not that I have anything against nice people—nice people are great, but we're talking about taking charge of your life, creating the reality you want, and maybe even raising the collective energy level of the world. These are huge concepts, and happen to all be connected. On the level of "where's my stuff?" these concepts work because the energy you're connecting to **is** the energy that all things are made of.

To "tune in and build up," you will need to find your own missing piece— the thing that fills up **your** energy supply. In order for your dreams, wishes, and goals to come to light, you'll need to develop a consistent method for filling up that supply.

Since you can't see your bank balance and there is no "energy ATM," how do you know how much you have?

A Totally Arbitrary Test to See How Much Energy You Have

Since there is not yet a gauge, scale, or graph for measuring your current amount of energy, take a moment right now and ask yourself the following questions:

- Do I feel "lucky" in my life, like I am in the flow and like things are working out without too much pushing?

- Do I regularly experience coincidences?

- Am I able to think of something or someone and have it (or them) appear relatively quickly?

- If I set goals, do "coincidences" start to happen right away to let me know I'm getting there, or does my life seem "dead in the water" and like I have to push every single thing I do?

If the answer to any of these questions is "no," chances are pretty good that you:

a) have energy, but are spending it on stuff you probably don't want like drama, bad situations, or compulsive habits, in which case you just need to re-train your mind to think about what you want; or

b) don't have much energy, and don't have a reliable method for "tapping in" to the energy within you so that your dreams and goals start to materialize regularly and you don't have to leave everything in your life up to some arbitrary, external thing called "Fate." As long as you're tapped in, you can direct the energy as you like.

Therefore, change the thoughts, or plug in the connection, or both. Simple, right?

Energy, Goals, and Methods—Many Pieces of the Puzzle

We can all name examples of people who seem to get everything they want. Certain celebrities are the most recognizable faces of this phenomenon, which is just the combination of a large amount of energy with a clear set of goals from early on, along with a reliable method of rebuilding and replenishing that energy. These people break through and have no trouble actualizing their goals and dreams, and as long as they stay focused, they stay on top.

***

What if you're not one of those people? What if there's no magic, and things aren't coming together for you, even after visualization? What if you're not accumulating wealth and success, no matter what you try?

Simple. You are not consistently connected with your own energy supply. No need for you to re-focus your goals, check your "vibrational frequency," or beat yourself over the head with a million repeated affirmations. Just build up the energy by meditating, feeling joy and gratitude for what you already have, and engaging in activities that make you feel good. Then, whatever you want is yours.

If you're still having trouble getting your head around this concept, that's okay. Here's another anecdote, just to put all of this in perspective. In terms of external energy (that is, the electricity that's in your house, that you plug things in to the wall socket to access and that you're using right now to shine light on this book), more progress was made in the late nineteenth century on this subject than in all previous years combined. According to Dragana Markovic in "The Second Industrial Revolution," "Through the work of such people as Nikola Tesla, Thomas Edison, Ottó Bláthy, George Westinghouse, Ernst Werner von Siemens, Alexander Graham Bell and Lord Kelvin, electricity was turned from a scientific curiosity into an essential tool for modern life."

It stands to reason that during our lifetime, the concept of turning energy into matter will become just as essential a tool for our lives. Consider this: little more than 100 years ago, Edison and Tesla were thought of as wizards because of their work with electricity, and now we take it for granted as one of the requirements/ conveniences of modern life. It is probable that 100 years from now, modern civilization will have such an understanding and knowledge of their own ability to turn energy into matter that this whole concept will be a "no brainer," and that our grandchildren will laugh at us about this. Because of a much greater understanding and shift of consciousness that is now occurring, life in the next century will be vastly different from what we currently see. Doesn't it benefit you to get on board with that revolution early?

Oh, and if you're curious, here are some other things that seemed totally impossible and crazy—until they happened:

- A man on the moon/ space travel in general

- Airplanes
- The sun being the center of the solar system
- The Earth not being flat
- Lasers
- An MRI machine that can see inside your body

Your Quantum Leap

In order to accept and start using these concepts, you're going to have to "think outside the box," as they say, and maybe change and let go of some of your beliefs as to where things like money come from, as well as developing an expanded understanding of (and connection to) a deeper part of yourself that you might not even know about yet. This is big stuff, and it's a big deal that you are willing to take this leap. If you're still with me, I'm glad. This discussion is definitely worth having, and it will benefit all of us if everyone just raises their energy supply just a little bit.

That's your part. Open-mindedness and a willingness to accept these new concepts as being possible (because they really, really work). On this end, I promise – no "hippie talk." No familiars, no angels, no dream interpretation. No psychics, no seeing dead people, no chakra balancing, and no vibrational resonance or tonality. That is to say, if you like doing one of these things or using one of these words, then great! That's just not what I'm doing here, so no one ends up feeling weird and hiding this book under a copy of **Rolling Stone** while they're at the dentist. Nope. Just straight talk about energy—as much as it is possible to speak clearly and plainly about things like energy, intention, visualization, and manifestation. By now, I'm sure you've read some other books on this concept, so you're probably familiar with the topics.

That By Any Other Name...

Here are some other words that have been used to describe what we'll call "your life energy":

- Spiritual substance
- Chi
- Prana
- Invisible Substance
- Presence
- Zero-point field
- Mind of God

- God Within
- Source energy
- Universal energy
- Universal mind

Right now, immediately if not sooner, stop visualizing, and start feeling your energy. It's just that simple.

3

Your Energy Supply—a Simple Concept, a Long Time in Coming

Energy is the only life and is from the Body, and Reason is the bound on outward circumference of Energy. Energy is Eternal Delight.

William Blake,
The Marriage of Heaven and Hell

Now that all of these big concepts have been laid out and you're thinking them over, I'm going to just give you a brief overview of how this discussion has been developing for a number of years, but it wasn't until now when science caught up with philosophy that we could actually use it in a practical way. Believe it or not, the concept of energy as the basis for your material possessions and experiences has been appearing in literature, some would say, since before the Bible. After all, Jesus **did** recommend meditating twice daily in order to connect to your own divinity. Some say that

Jesus' "Christ Consciousness" was what allowed him to perform miracles, meaning he was so in touch with his inner energy flow that he was easily able to do things like feeding the masses by multiplying bread and fish and that sort of thing.

However, since the mention of Jesus Christ is so laden with different meanings and associations for so many, we're going to just talk about this "energy" on the most neutral level possible. As you're digesting these new concepts and trying to locate the energy within you so that you may harness it and visualize it into a new car, let's turn our attention to the real "secret" inside Napoleon Hill's groundbreaking work "Think and Grow Rich", which has sold something like 50 million copies since its original publication in 1937, as well as to some other "personal achievement" classics. For years, people have been saying this "secret" is really the law of attraction, but a close examination of the text provides evidence that Hill is really going much deeper.

In case you haven't read "Think and Grow Rich," it's the culmination of Napoleon Hill's work with Andrew Carnegie and of his interviews with over 500 successful and noteworthy people ranging from Henry Ford to

Thomas Edison to Andrew Carnegie himself. As it turns out, this book was maybe 100 years ahead of its time in terms of its comprehension and reference to what we now know to be energy, and of the direction of this energy through one's thoughts. "Think and Grow Rich" is included as one of the free bonuses for this book, so definitely go over and download it at http://wealthfromwithinbook.com/resources

Just so you know, Napoleon Hill studied under Carnegie for more than twenty-five years, and was apparently also reading all of the "success through thought direction" literature of the "New Thought" movement of the late nineteenth century (which included Wallace Wattles, Thomas Troward, and Charles Haanel). In fact, in 1919 Hill wrote a letter to Charles Haanel, thanking him for "The Master Key System," in which Hill says "My present success and the success which has followed my work as President of the Napoleon Hill Institute is due largely to the principles laid down in 'The Master-Key System.'"

And what is the primary topic of "The Master-Key System?" None other than energy and its direction by the mind:

> *The whole world is on the eve of a new consciousness, a new power and a new realization of the resources within the self. The last century saw the most magnificent material and spiritual power.*
>
> *Physical science has resolved matter into molecules, molecules into atoms, atoms into energy, and it has remained for Sir Ambrose Fleming, in an address before the Royal Institution, to resolve this energy into mind. He says "In its ultimate essence, energy may be incomprehensible by us except as an exhibition of the direct operation of that which we call Mind or Will.*
>
> (Charles Haanel, "The Master Key System," 1912)

In the very first line of the Introduction to "Think and Grow Rich", Hill tells his readers: "In every chapter of this book, mention has been made of the money-making secret which has made fortunes for hundreds of exceedingly wealthy men whom I have carefully analyzed over a long period of years. This secret was brought to my attention by Andrew Carnegie." Hill goes on to say that this secret is mentioned more than a hundred times in "Think and Grow Rich", and that if you are ready to put it into use, you will recognize this secret at least once in every chapter. This "secret" that Hill is referring to is not only the "law of attraction," but even more fundamentally, the energy behind it.

Now, let's go back to the original research and publication of "Think and Grow Rich", which occurred between 1908 and 1928. During this time, Hill's work with Carnegie and other multimillionaires coincides with innovations in electrical engineering, and it was just becoming commonplace to have electricity in your home and to own a car with an internal combustion engine, but advances in quantum physics had not come into the mainstream yet.

Since any understanding of "energy" is limited at this point to what's going on with electricity, there is room for the "science of personal achievement" in the public consciousness, and that's about it. Advances in quantum physics, biology, and metaphysics won't come until the latter half of the twentieth century, and so

Napoleon Hill is sitting on a huge breakthrough in the understanding of energy. Unfortunately, because science hadn't caught up yet, **there literally was no vocabulary to communicate these concepts**.

Because Hill knows this message will really help people if they come to understand what he's learned, he embeds this breakthrough into a book about "personal achievement" and a "positive mental attitude" like a time capsule. Today, we look at it again with our new understanding and information, and we find:

> *This statement is of tremendous importance...every one of the billions of cells of your body and every atom of matter, began as an intangible form of energy...When you begin with the thought impulse, desire, to accumulate money, you are drafting into your service the same "stuff" that nature used in creating this earth, and every material form in the universe, including the body and brain in which the thought impulses function.*

Wow! Add 70 + years of progress, scientific understanding of energy, and your ability to feel this energy within yourself, and it becomes clear that the real secret of "Think and Grow Rich" goes far beyond the law of attraction, into a metaphysical realm that we are only just beginning to understand.

And, although "Think and Grow Rich" is certainly the most well-known of these texts, this is by no means the first reference to what until now has been called everything from "God spirit" to "our invisible supply" over the past 2,000 years. Author John Randolph Price ("Superbeings") traces what he calls the "principle of self sufficiency" from ancient Kabbalah teachings through Gnostic practices and into the Bible in his excellent "40 Day Prosperity Program" book, which I definitely recommend. The only drawback to this program (developed by Price in 1987) is that it calls this energy "Spirit of God" and leans heavily toward the religious, which might be off-putting if you're trying to think of it just as "your own energy" to avoid religious connotation or resistance from your own upbringing. That is to say, if you went to church as a kid and really loved it, you will probably love the books. If you have negative associations, you might not.

To further understand how this concept has been "hiding in plain sight" in literature, let's go back to some highlights of the "New Thought" movement, starting with "Thoughts Are Things," which was written in 1889 by Prentice Mulford.

Mulford talks mainly about directing your thoughts and being in the "current of right attitude," but midway through the book, he mentions an "unseen element" in this passage:

> *Your spirit as part of the great whole has the germ, and waiting for fruition, the same power. Christ, through power of concentrating the unseen element of his thought, could turn that unseen element into the seen, and materialize food—loaves and fishes. That is a power inherent in every spirit, and every spirit is growing in such a power.*

Then there's "Our Invisible Supply: How to Obtain," by Frances Larimer Warner, published in 1907. Warner is discussing not focusing on money (or lack thereof), because doing so stops the "unseen supply" from which money is derived.

> *For surely as we pinch and hold the symbol, just so surely do we hold the flow of the unseen supply which explains "without faith it is impossible to please God," because Good cannot flow as supply*

when we ourselves are holding it back with a taut rein.

Wallace Wattles says in again it his 1910 book "The Science of Getting Rich":

Everything you see on earth is made from one original substance, out of which all things proceed... There is no limit to the supply of Formless Stuff, or Original Substance. The universe is made out of it...between the forms of the visible universe are permeated by Original Substance; with the formless Stuff, with the raw material of all things. Ten thousand times as much as has been made might still be made, and even then we should not have exhausted the supply of universal raw material. Thought is the only power which can produce tangible results from the Formless Substance.

From there, we move on to Genevieve Behrend, who quotes Thomas Troward in her book "Your Invisible Power" (1921) as saying:

If we can get at the working principle which is producing these results, we can very quickly and easily give it personal application. First, we find that the thought of originating life or Spirit about itself is its simple awareness of its own being and this produced a primary ether, a universal substance out of which everything in the world must grow."

Behrend takes Troward's conclusions even further, adding that "Before you would entertain the idea of making a mental picture of your desire as being at all practical, you must have some idea of your being, of your 'I am.'"

Simultaneously, Neville Goddard has picked up this idea and done extensive work on it, publishing works such as "The Power of Awareness," "Your Faith is Your Fortune," and "Awakened Imagination."

In his influential 1961 work, "The Law and the Promise," he says:

> *The purpose of this... book is to show, through actual true stories, how imagining creates reality. Science progresses by way of hypotheses tentatively tested and afterwards accepted or rejected according to the facts of experience. The claim that imagining creates reality needs no more consideration than is*

*allowed by science. It proves itself in performance...
When man solves the mystery of imagining, he will
have discovered the secret of causation, and that is:
Imagining creates reality. Therefore, the man who is
aware of what he is imagining knows what he is
creating; realizes more and more that the drama of
life is imaginal — not physical. All activity is at
bottom imaginal. An awakened Imagination works
with a purpose. It creates and conserves the
desirable, and transforms or destroys the
undesirable.*

*We are all filled with pent-up substance, energy and
divine ability which wishes to work for us, through
us, and about us. Psychologists declare that the
average person uses only about 10% of his mind
power. Medical authorities claim that the average
person uses only about 25% of his physical
power...Surely there is great power within you for
prosperous living through releasing deliberate
thoughts, feelings and mental pictures of success,
prosperity and riches. As you do so, your rich
thoughts, feelings, and mental pictures are radiated
outward into the rich, powerful ethers of this
universe, where they make contact with the rich,
universal substance.*

Around this same time, another "New Thought" writer, Catherine Ponder, is also expressing this idea:

God's rich supply is all around you universally, as well as innately within you...but that rich supply must be contacted and used. Your mind is your connecting link with it. Your attitudes, your mental concepts, beliefs and outlook are your connecting link with God's rich substance and your access to it. Begin making contact with the rich, universal substance around you and within you by declaring often: "I stir up the gifts of God within me and around me, and I am blessed on every hand with happiness, success, and true achievement. Just by declaring this idea, you will begin stirring up the riches of the universe, attracting them to you and expressing them through you.

("Dynamic Laws of Prosperity," 1962)

Clearly, the underlying message of all of these influential works is not just "thoughts become things," but "thoughts create things out of our own supply of energy." And while it makes perfect sense that the main conclusion of any analysis of these texts before now would conclude that all of these authors are talking just about the law of attraction, a closer look shows us that the discussion of energy (not just law of attraction) has been going on for some time, though we are just now catching up to what it really means in terms of the unified field, quantum physics, and practical applications for our lives.

Now that we've looked at some historical references to the need for the energy connection before visualization, let's turn our attention (literally) to how to find that connection within yourself and start building it up. Next stop: meditation!

4

Connect, and Build Up!

That's the power of meditation: it gives you an opportunity to make conscious contact with your Source and to regain the power of your Source. The power of your Source is the power to sustain and create life; it's the power to perform miracles. It's the power to live at a level of awareness that goes beyond just ordinary human consciousness or ordinary human awareness.

Dr. Wayne Dyer

So, how do you access the energy within yourself? How do you get it flowing? And, how can you build up enough so that it starts creating the life that you want?

To consistently create your life through visualization, affirmations, declarations, or whatever other method you choose, you must develop a system wherein you connect to the energy within you. Ultimately, your goal is to stay connected to that "life energy" feeling as much of the time as possible. Consider this state like an "Energy Factory" mode, in which you are aware of your own energy (therefore making more of it).

The first step is setting up a regular practice of meditation, or (if you think the word "meditation" sounds boring or you have a negative association), "a regularly kept time to connect with your own energy so that you can start building it up," is to schedule some quiet time during the day where you can relax and clear your mind. The more time you spend in this state, the more energy you will have, and the more quickly you will be able to manifest your goals.

Before your thinking mind/ego starts with the excuses ("Meditation is boring! I can't do it! It's too hard! It's too time-consuming!"), consider this interesting fact: *all* of the law of attraction experts in "The Secret" practice some form of meditation! In fact, meditation is mentioned briefly in the book:

> *Without exception, every teacher in this book uses meditation as a daily practice... Meditation quiets*

your mind, helps you control your thoughts, and revitalizes your body.

(Rhonda Byrne, "The Secret")

Meditation doesn't just quiet the mind and help you control your thoughts—it's also a powerful way to build up your supply of energy so that your visualizations will have something to back them up. Energy supply (augmented by meditation) is certainly a factor in the success of all of the teachers in "The Secret," and should be for you as well. Do as they do!

Using meditation to build and develop your connection to and supply of energy doesn't have to be difficult, but (just like anything worth doing) it is going to take some work, and some setting up. If you already have a meditation practice that's working for you, I would recommend that in addition to "quieting your mind," you also turn your attention to contemplation of your own energy, because it is really this deeper practice that builds up supply. This can work even if you stop and check in with yourself at times throughout the day. Whatever works for you!

Meditation: Not What You Think

People who are devout meditators **do** have greater amounts of patience, lower blood pressure, and are perhaps more able to deal with the stresses of life. If that's what you're after, it's fine to just quiet your mind a few times a day by sitting in the silence and trying to quiet your mind for twenty minutes (or more) per day, or just take multiple "time outs" during the day where you clear your head and re-connect with your energy supply.

If what you're looking for is a metaphysical breakthrough, traditional "quiet your mind" type meditation is most likely not going to get you there (though there are certainly exceptions to this statement, as with everything). What you need is a reliable way of connecting with your own life force through focused meditation—an "Inspired Meditation." During Inspired Meditation, your mind won't be wandering, because it has a job—to focus on the energy/life force within you. Of course, since you've never done this before, it might take a little while to build up to the twenty minutes-twice-daily routine that is recommended as a basis for building up energy, but you will find that it's not nearly as difficult as just sitting there. When you start to observe and connect with your own energy, an amazing thing happens—you start to feel more comfortable in this "meditative" state than in your regular life. I'm calling this practice "inspired meditation," since I want to make sure we're clear—no "dead mediation" where you just "quiet your mind!"

Inspired Meditation—Simple Instructions

- Sit or lie down in a comfortable position where you can be aware of your whole body. Put your hands together (or very close together) so you can more easily feel the current of energy flowing through your body.

- Close your eyes, and take a few deep breaths. Let your mind "spin down" from whatever it was engaged in before you entered your energy-building time. Count back from 100 slowly if this helps you enter a more relaxed state. Don't go to sleep!

- With the specific intention of connecting with your own inner energy (or "spirit"), repeat a phrase (you will need to experiment until you find one that works for you). Some that have worked for me include:

"I can feel my energy"
"I can feel the spirit of God"
"I invite the universal One into my life."

- Let your mind focus on your phrase and repeat it over and over again, and soon, you will start to experience your own energy. It might feel like "the chills" that you get when you hear something inspiring, or maybe you'll feel a slight tingling or heat somewhere in your body. There is no right or wrong feeling, and no "test" to make sure you're doing it right. You are the best judge of whether you're feeling something, and you will know when you are feeling connected. It's that simple. Maybe you've never really taken the time to notice it before, but once you do, you will be surprised at how strong it feels! The most common place to start feeling this energy is in your hands and feet, but after a few minutes, you will definitely be feeling it everywhere.

- Stay in this state for as long as is comfortable at that time (again, you might need to build up). Your goal is to not only perform this meditative process on a twice-daily basis (for at least twenty minutes) to insure the constant flow of energy into your life, but to reset your "default" state so that you can more easily slip back into this awareness and be allowing more of this energy (which will become money and success) all throughout your day.

You definitely can do this on your own, but in case you're the kind of person who prefers a "guided meditation" type thing, we have a list on www.wealthfromwithinbook.com . You should absolutely do whatever works best for you, and no one can tell you which one is exactly right.

Other Forms of Meditation to Try

If you haven't yet found a meditation that works for you, don't give up! Keep trying until you find something that stirs the spirit within you. Only you will know what that is! Here are some other options:

Japa Meditation

This is the "AH" meditation popularized by Wayne Dyer in his CD, "Meditations for Manifesting," and his book "Getting in the Gap." Japa Meditation, where one repeats the "AH" sound of the name of God as a mantra, is said to be "one of the most effective forms of meditation," and I suspect this is because the chanting of the "AH" sound stirs up the energy inside you and makes you aware of it. I personally have not been able to get into this form because the chant makes me feel self-conscious, even if I am alone. But, definitely try it— it could be the thing that works for you!

Silva Method Life Accelerator

The "Silva Method" of meditation, which involves putting your brain into the "Alpha" level several times per day, is the product of several decades of research by hypnosis pioneer Jose Silva. His legacy is carried on by his family now that he's passed away. It's a good system and a good value for the whole program ($97 plus a bunch of free bonuses if you get the download-only version), and it has built-in audio for guided meditation, learning tools, anchoring, and relaxation. For more information, visit www.silvamethod.com.

Vipanassa

If you're ready for the ultimate retreat, you might want to consider Vipanassa meditation. The Vipanassa method of meditation has retreat centers all over the United States (and the world) where their intense, ten-day program with ten hours of daily meditation and silence will surely be the most intense experience of your life. Vipanassa is a charitable organization, so the retreats are free. Visit www.vipanassa.org for more information and locations.

Transcendental Meditation

The Beatles did it. David Lynch swears by it. Jerry Seinfeld has apparently been doing it since he was 19. It's been around since 1958, with millions of devotees around the world. The David Lynch Foundation is working to bring this type of meditation to millions of school-age kids. There is a fee for proper instruction with a certified TM instructor. If you are curious, definitely visit www.tm.org to see if Transcendental Meditation might be right for you.

What's the Ideal Meditation Schedule for You?

The standard "how long do I meditate?" answer is

usually: twenty minutes, twice a day. This is easy to remember, is surprisingly easy to work up to, and builds a fantastic amount of energy once you get on a roll.

Ideally, you will be able to do your first meditation in the morning, before you check your email or get into the shower and zone out, only to realize it's 3:00 and you've been on autopilot all day.

First, though, get out of bed. If you try to put yourself in a meditative, energy-building state when you are lying down first thing in the morning, you will probably go back to sleep, and no one wants that. It is tempting to jump right into your day, but remember, wealth =connectedness to energy, which makes it 100 % worth getting up early to work on this. Think about it this way: you're getting paid to meditate!

Re-Training Your Brain to Form New Habits
Just like forming any other kind of habit, once you start to see the benefits of a regular practice of inspired meditation, (the crazy coincidences, the money showing up from random places, and the things that start just falling into place), you will be more and more motivated

to build this habit. Think of it like building up a muscle—you wouldn't go to a gym and try to do that in one day, especially if you had never been active or lifted weights before. You'd start with a two-pounder and build up from there with consistent action. Well, if a constant connection to spiritual and metaphysical consciousness is our ultimate, 500-pound bench press goal, just accepting these truths and embarking on a plan of meditation is our two-pound weight. This is something you can start now—right now—that will go a long way toward building that amazing life you have in your mind.

Meditation, in case you're wondering, has been around for 5,000 years, and has been used to augment and/or deepen the study or practice of every religion that has ever existed. People all throughout history have extolled its virtues, as everything from a sure-fire method of relaxation to a cure for hypertension and depression to the way to deepen or develop your relationship to God (or your spiritual life). For the purposes of this book (and with the most advanced understanding of energy and quantum physics that has ever been), we're going to use meditation as a method to literally contact and build up the energy that is the basis of not only our life circumstances, but the stuff that we see in our reality.

"It Seems Too Simple to Be True"

Make no mistake—the work you're doing now, the work of connecting to and building up your energy, is going to be some of the most challenging work you're going to do in your life—at first. At first it will seem like nothing is happening, that the whole practice of meditation is pointless, and that you'd be better off just "working hard." You might have to really wrestle with your mind for several years before it fully accepts this concept, and there's no shame in that. Some people are stuck on this point for years.

Who Else Meditates?

OK, now you're probably going to want some examples of people who have clearly used meditation (either knowingly or unknowingly) to build up massive amounts of energy, which they then turned into money and/or success.

Ask and ye shall receive!

- Oprah Winfrey, world's richest woman and media mogul, has admitted to being a "big meditator." I'm guessing she practices every day, but maybe she's so good at it she's just in that state all the time.
- Eckhart Tolle
- Dr. Wayne Dyer
- Richard Gere, a movie star for decades, has been practicing Buddhist meditation for about 35 years.
- Goldie Hawn, who is said to have a meditation room in her house.
- Russell Simmons
- Tina Turner, who famously credits Buddhist meditation for getting her through her abusive relationship with Ike Turner. Also, her solo career took off after she started practicing.

Still not convinced? Here are some other names you might recognize, all of whom are said to have practiced meditation:

Orlando Bloom, Shania Twain, Sting, Sheryl Crow, Bill Ford of Ford Motors, Al Gore, Deepak Chopra, Henry

David Thoreau, Gandhi, Stevie Wonder, The Dalai Lama, Jack Canfield, Benjamin Franklin, Herbie Hancock, Leonard Cohen, George Harrison, John Lennon, Paul McCartney, Ringo Starr, Ezra Pound, Madonna, Sting, Herbie Hancock, Moby, Jack Kerouac, and Allen Ginsberg.

Bottom line: meditation is not a luxury—it's a necessary building block of your successful life, just like brushing your teeth, working out, setting goals, and taking action. Get started as soon as possible!

5

Keep the Flow Going

Once you've got your meditation practice established and you can regularly feel the flow of energy into your life, it is important to also engage in activities that you think are fun and that make you feel alive. Simply put, joy increases your amount of energy, which makes everything in your life work better.

"Do What You Love and the Money Will Follow"

Doing what you love or what you feel "inspired" to do will connect you with your own energy, which you can then direct into money in your life. I don't think the "...and the money will follow" part always means you will get paid for doing the actual thing you love, but it does mean that money will come into your life in some way, because of the energy you've built up by doing your inspired thing. That is to say, it's not necessarily the activity itself, but the energy accumulated by the love of doing that thing, that is building up the energy.

Here Are Some Energy-Building Activities (feel free to add some of your own!):

- Singing
- Dancing
- Laughing
- Charitable work (giving unto others)
- Engaging in any activity you "love," even if you have the belief that it's "just a hobby."
- Spending time with children or animals
- Attending live events like concerts, art shows, live sporting events, or any group activity where others share your interests. Collective energy can be very high at these types of places!
- Cooking or eating with friends
- Traveling
- Spending time in "high energy" places, like deserts, forests, or the beach.
- Exercising

This is really just a list of generally enjoyable activities. It is up to you to figure out what "stirs up" your inner energy, so that you can expand your awareness of this energy that is building your life around you. Everyone has their own things that give them great joy. Find that thing, feel the energy of what that joy feels like inside you, and then take that with you and focus on it in order to multiply it in your life.

Connecting with the "Presence" or the Now

An excellent book on this subject is "The Power of Now," by Eckhart Tolle, who is also the author of "A New Earth," "Stillness Speaks," and several other books on this topic. Tolle's main purpose is the evolution of consciousness, but his methods are also very effective in building up energy to apply it to your goals, since staying in the flow does build energy.

Tolle does not make this direct "building up energy" connection in his work, probably because he has experienced a sort of "ego death," meaning he has very little (if any) attachment to the material world and is now more concerned with raising consciousness in general as opposed to using this energy to make your life work better. Several other authors describe this state, including the Dalai Lama and Dr. Jill Bolte Taylor, the brain scientist who suffered a stroke and then went on to become the well-known author of the spiritually-based book "A Stroke of Genius." I like these books, but one issue I have is that I am not (yet) free of ego, and so I feel like these authors are on the "other side" of the ego battle describing what it's like, rather than giving me practical steps to get there. I've found that if you take their work and simply apply the "supply and demand" energy formula to it, this can be a very useful method.

There are several good ways to ensure that energy-building habits become a permanent part of your life. Remember, without a reliable source of tapping into and building up your own energy, it will be difficult to "make" things happen by effort alone or through visualization. Your work is connecting to the energy of the universe!

1. Practice meditation. I can't say this enough. If you haven't already, start up a meditation practice that makes you feel you are connected and getting the energy flowing, and stick with it until you've built up to twenty minutes, twice a

day. You will see the results! Meditation is the building block of your life!

2. Make a playlist. Get books on tape, or subscribe to Oprah's "Spirit Channel" podcast. Have something inspirational playing in the background of your life at all times, at least for the first thirty days, just to remind you to re-connect with the flow of the universe.

3. Speaking of Oprah, take the "New Earth" course done by Oprah and Eckhart Tolle. With your new knowledge of energy as the basis for your life, you will be able to easily understand the subject matter, and taking this course (it's free and you can get the materials online), will solidify the concepts and keep you connected to the flow of energy in your life.

4. Go on a retreat. If you have the time, you might want to head out by yourself for as long as is feasible, preferably to a place that is quiet and surrounded by nature. This doesn't have to cost a fortune; in fact, camping or simply hiking or walking outdoors will work just fine. By clearing

your mind and circumstances of the distractions of everyday life, you make it easier for your mind to accept the truth that your own energy is the basis for your life, and (as you've probably concluded by now) it is much easier to get into the habit of feeling this energy when you're in nature and surrounded by silence. Go for a walk in the desert!

5. Practice mindfulness. The idea behind the concept of "mindfulness" is that you bring the "flow" you experience while meditating into ALL aspects of your life, from working to washing dishes to playing with your kids. If this concept interests you, you might want to pick up "Miracle of Mindfulness" by Thich Nhat Hahn, which addresses feeling that presence in everyday activities. Jon Kabat-Zinn is also a great resource for meditations on mindfulness. You can find his books and CDs on www.soundstrue.com, and some of his guided meditations are on YouTube.

Important Steps to Further Cement Your New Habit

- **Turn off the news** Part of the reason this economic meltdown has gotten so bad is because of collective consciousness focusing on fearful, negative circumstances. When you focus on what's going on now, you take your attention off of your own energy, which unplugs the connection or flow of energy into your life. Ironically, if the millions of people who are glued to *Mad Money* and hoping for a turnaround would turn off the television and put their focus on their own energy (through meditation and mindfulness), the actual turnaround would come that much faster. Also ironically, the more you focus in on yourself and your own life force, the less you care about external circumstances. And, as we all know, the less you care, the more you have. Uninterrupted flow!

- **Avoid Drama** We all know people who love to complain, and to whom crazy stuff is always happening. For instance, I know a person who always has a crazy roommate, and she is always re-hashing the stories of what they've done and how she just can't believe it. She's one of those people who attracts drama, and every time I see her (which isn't very often if I can help it), she has a long story of her latest saga. I suggest that if you know one of these people (or you are one), you make a conscious effort to avoid getting sucked in to craziness, for the simple reason that these situations are distracting you from focusing on your own energy, which is making it harder for you to achieve your goals.

Avoiding drama and craziness will come more easily the more you are able to realize your own energetic self-sufficiency. The more good results you get, the less you will want to involve yourself in external circumstances that block the flow of energy into your life. Avoiding people who seem to be in constant conflict with the world is helpful, though as you solidify your own good habits, these types of people will naturally be removed from your life, as if by magic.

Keep the Faith

The concept of having faith, or believing that you will receive, really just has to do with an understanding of your own supply of energy and how to build and direct it. Focus on your energy supply through the practices of meditation and the other energy-builders (like joy, gratitude, and love), be clear about what you want, and you will see the results.

Practice Gratitude

Gratitude is all over "The Secret," and authentic gratitude (in my experience) is not only one of the most powerful energy-building activities, but one of the easiest things you can do to start it flowing and keep your mind occupied. Make a list of 100 things you are grateful for—your health, your job, your friends, your dog, your kids, or anything else that comes to mind. If you make gratitude a habit and remind yourself throughout the day of all the things you are grateful for, you will be in a better mood and be building up your energy, and that is good for everyone. Get out a notebook and make a list right now!

This is a lot of information, but hopefully you can take one or more of these things and integrate them into your life, finding new ways to connect to that flow of energy. You can do it!

6

Set Your Goals, and Visualize Them

Creative visualization is the technique of using your imagination to create what you want in your life...You are already using it every day, every minute in fact.

Shakti Gawain, Creative Visualization

Finally: Visualization!

So much has already been written on this topic, it would be ridiculous to think I could fit all of the subtle nuances into one chapter. But, I do know one thing: visualization (at least for me) cannot work without a solid connection to internal energy.

It is very important to understand that when you visualize something, that thing is actually being ***formed*** out of your own supply of energy. You have built that energy up by acknowledging and connecting with it on a regular basis (through meditation, mindfulness, or whatever other method you've found to connect with your own sense of aliveness). Visualization is just that—you are creating the thing you are visualizing, and if you're in the flow of energy, you can be sure that the thing you're visualizing will be with you shortly.

Does this mean things are going to go down exactly the way your thinking mind is picturing them? Probably not. But, as we've already determined, your thinking mind doesn't know everything—really it's just in charge of taking the blueprints of what you want down the hall to the energy factory. However, you can be relatively certain that if you have a reliable "flow" of energy going and a way of creatively visualizing your goal and how it's going to feel when you get it, it's going to come your way somehow. Hey, even though you have this new piece of the puzzle, there still has to be some mystery left, right?

Set Your Goals

Even if you're one of the lucky people born with a great deal of energy, it's all just floating around out there as potential until you make up your mind as to what you really want. The world is full of people who meditate regularly, then sabotage themselves with limiting beliefs about "the way life should be," with no expectations or any real goals. While you have a direct line into "the source" of energy and are good at accumulating it, your lack of focus and/or discipline means that you've probably experienced a significant amount of turbulence in your life as you try to decide what it is that you really want, or as you try to overcome whatever voice in your head that's telling you "you can't do it," or many cycles of "having it all" and then "losing it all." You *can* do it, you *are* doing it, and the more you work on it, the better you're going to get.

Some might call people like this underachievers, but in reality they're just people who are sitting on a giant bank account but who are afraid to write checks (or don't even know about the account at all). If you have a regular meditation or yoga practice (or a reliable way of feeling real joy or connection), but you have no real goals or aspirations in your life, do yourself a favor and just decide what you want. Now that you know that all of your desires are formed out of your own supply of energy, it shouldn't be a problem to overcome any limiting beliefs like "that's not possible!" You have all the tools in place. You just need to teach yourself to set goals and think big. This is a totally solvable problem, and you will be amazed at what happens!

If you haven't set any goals for your life, now's the time! Right now, take out a notebook and brainstorm some goals. Write down some concrete stuff, like "one million dollars" or "a new house" or "a job I love," or "my soul mate." You really want to have some specific places for all that energy to go, so it helps to make the goal list as specific as possible. Think about it: what do you really want? While you're making the list, also make a note about how these things are going to make you feel, like, "I will be really satisfied when I have achieved my goal of being a multimillionaire." This list will come in handy later when you're actually doing the visualization.

If you're like me, the first thing your brain does after you set your goals is to try to think of ways to get there. At this point, let's stop and have another discussion of energy supply and the way things work.

Focus on the Goal and the Energy, Not How You'll Get There

Let me dispel a popular myth for you, to save you countless, thankless hours of sending emails, bugging people, or trying to brainstorm new ideas. Personally, before I had a realization about energy and started working on that, I worked about as "hard" as one person could work. Here is the one thing I learned from all that work and struggle:

You cannot "make" your goals happen!

These words are not meant to depress or discourage you—not one bit. They are merely to advise you, beyond a shadow of a doubt that without attention to your energy "bank account," you are not going to be able to make yourself into a Brad Pitt-style movie star, or a bestselling author like J.K. Rowling. A quantum leap of this level cannot be achieved by ego-based activities alone with no attention paid to building up energy. This is why people spend years trying to make themselves into authors, actors, or entrepreneurs, only to find that they can never catch a break.

Unfortunately, the very act of "trying," or "trying to push that rock up that hill," is sapping the very energy that could be getting you closer to your goal. Yes, this is an inexact science, and yes, you are free to not believe anything I'm saying. But, think of all the people you know who are constantly trying to "get things going" in their lives, and are infusing everything and everyone around them with the energy of desperation that no one can stand to be around—an energy that screams, "Nothing is working! I know it's not, but I'm trying it anyway!"

If you're at that point, stop. Just stop. Stop right now! You are bankrupting yourself of energy by trying to do all the heavy lifting yourself. This is not going to work, and if you eventually manage to eke out some measure of success by using your ego/ thinking mind alone, you will have left yourself so exhausted and depleted, you will almost certainly find this success to be empty, since it can never give you back the energy that you spent. It will feel artificial, and awful—like you had no faith and you had to force it. This is not the way of real success, so you'll be relieved to know that no amount of struggling or forcing it is likely to do you any good. Life is not meant to be hard work, in the sense that you've come to know it. "Hard work" is fine when we're talking about our creative lives, but if you're noticing that you work really hard at your job and/or your goals and still nothing seems to be moving, it's time to re-assess and focus back in on building that energy!

Trying to "push the rock up the hill," so to speak, without using energy as the strength behind it almost always backfires, meaning it can be done, but it does not feel good, and it usually comes with a price. Do yourself a favor—put the attention you're spending on "making the effort" back on the energy/ spirit within you, and you will be amazed at the results.

Visualization: See, Feel, or Experience it In Your Mind

Once you're in the practice of sitting in a meditative practice twice a day, take a few minutes at the end of that time to focus your attention on sending that energy to the things on your "goal list." The most effective way to do this is by thinking about how you best learn or experience this in the world, then using your imagination in that way when you think about your goals.

If you're a "feeling" type person, you can do this by referring back to the feelings you've associated with each goal. If you're more visual, try to really picture yourself in the scene, including all the things that would be in that scene. If you're a "written words" type of person, try writing your goals in a notebook.

Visualization, Step by Step

1. Sit or lie down, count back from ten to relax

2. Do your meditation (twenty minutes of connecting with and building up your own energy)

3. At the end of your meditation session, picture your goal in a way that seems true to you, so that you can actually get a sense for what it's going to be like when you get it. Only you know what works for you. Keep trying different things until you feel a connection!

4. Let it Go. This is the "detachment" part of visualization/ goal setting, where you go about your business and allow your energy to fulfill your vision. This is a tough one for most people

(including me), because I tend to want to "overwork" the goal, burning up energy along the way. This step requires faith. Work on it with me, won't you?

Simplify, and Take Inspired Action

Now that you've got your "work," meaning meditation and other energy-building practices, and you're focusing that energy toward your goals, ask yourself: what action can you take toward your goal that will move things forward without pushing it and falling out of that "in the flow" place?

This seems like an odd question, especially since most people on this path of personal development tend to be what is traditionally referred to as "overachievers" or "Type A personalities." Really, though, once you establish your connection with the universal energy and set it into motion with some method of visualization, you will find that things are easier and require much less strategic planning and "heavy lifting" on your part. It's not that you won't have to work hard, but it definitely won't feel like you're pushing the rock up the hill anymore.

Right now, while this concept and these new habits settle in, it would be great if you could pare your daily life and efforts down as much as possible to include only the "bare necessities." That is to say, if it's going to make you feel really bad if you don't make some "effort" toward your goals every day, then by all means make a list and accomplish some things on it. On one level, you do need to keep things in order and make sure you're taking action toward your goals. However, if you have a whole "take over the world" scheme that involves a lot of pulleys and ropes, and you run around all day like a chicken with your head cut off, trying to "get successful" or "make something out of yourself" (so much so that you don't have time to meditate or even accomplish many of the things on the list), now is the time to put that on hold while you begin to find space for these new concepts (as well as the space to allow energy into your life). You will probably find that the more energy you build up, the less "heavy lifting" you'll actually have to do.

A golden rule for this: if you're taking action and it feels like you're forcing it, stop! Better to wait for inspiration to hit so that you can take effective action. Until then, simplify, meditate, and let it go!

No, it's not easy. When you're first learning to stay in the "flow" of energy all the time, it seems like you're either in one place or the other. Either you're in your "higher consciousness," meaning you are meditating or are engaged in an activity you enjoy (thereby building the energy in your life), or you're in the "practical consciousness" where you're paying bills or doing business on the phone. Think of it like a hose. When you're actively engaging your "God consciousness," water (or energy) is flowing out at full velocity. However, the minute you slip back into "practical consciousness," a kink appears in the hose, and the energy slows to a drip. Eventually, using the techniques in this book, you will develop the ability to be in both states of your mind at once. Some spiritual teachers and authors call this mindfulness, or consciously bringing presence into everything you do.

You and Your Money

Even after you get the hang of building up the energy, a very important step in the manifestation and realization of money in your life is the successful clearing out of negative thoughts, patterns, and associations concerning money. If you find yourself feeling negative feelings toward rich people or saying things like, "Oh, I don't need a lot of money—I'm an artist," or "I just wasn't raised with a lot of money, so I'm not comfortable with it," then this is definitely an area that must be cleaned up before wealth and abundance can start to flow your way, since that new storehouse of energy needs to be directed by your thoughts in order to materialize in your life.

To learn much more in this area, pick up the excellent book, "Secrets of the Millionaire Mind" by T. Harv Eker (a fellow meditator and multi-millionaire!). It's very straight-forward, can be read frequently, and has exercises to help you clear out any mental roadblocks you may have with your financial "blueprint," as Eker calls it. Change your blueprint, and all your new-found energy supply will flow into a picture of financial success in your life!

Don't stop with that book, though—once you've cleared out the old rubble of counter-productive thoughts and built a new pattern in your mind, you still need your energy in order to actually get the money into your life. Everything starts with energy!

If you've read the book and are confident that you don't have any of these money landmines holding you back, I would still encourage you to get your finances in order by taking the following simple steps:

1. Pay off debt.

2. Learn about sources of passive income.

3. Educate yourself about compound interest and investments, and set up a savings account/retirement account/portfolio. Make room for the money in your life, and it will come!

4. Start a new notebook of "million dollar ideas" that will hit you when you've built up energy.

Why do these things? Simple: If your goal is wealth of any kind, you first need to lay the groundwork for wealth by cleaning up what's in your reality (what you have now). This is mainly so you don't have to think about it, and so you can devote your full attention to building energy (which you will then direct to become money). If you are distracted by the fact that you should be paying off your debt and investing for the future (yes, you should be), it's going to be even harder for you to build up that energy, and harder to get into the "I am a multimillionaire" visualization when you know that you have a huge mental block when it comes to your finances. In other words, don't hope for a miracle of energy to get you out of debt. Set things up now and start working on a plan, open a savings account and get your head on straight about money. Once you've got stuff in place and start building up the energy and directing it towards prosperity, you will be shocked at how quickly things will start to happen. Soon you won't even need that old plan anymore, because everything will be paid off and your net worth will be growing by the day.

If for some reason you don't get into T. Harv Eker's book (fair enough), here are some other excellent books that will help you address this totally critical issue before you move on in the process.

- One Minute Millionaire
- Any of Suze Orman's books
- Many of Tony Robbins programs

Cleaning House

It is true that "thoughts become things," so as you connect with and build your supply of energy, you will want to also "clean house" of the negative beliefs and thoughts that might be holding you back. For instance, it would be a shame if you did all that work connecting to your energy and really feeling the presence within you, then consistently focused on (and therefore created) negative circumstances because you had a counter-productive belief like "artists should be poor." Some spiritual guru types will call this kind of thing an "energetic block," but since we are trying to be as down to earth as possible here, let's say that if you keep thinking "artists should be poor" because that's what your parents told you, then you will consistently make decisions that do not allow a lot of money into your life. It is a good idea to get those out of the way so you're not holding yourself back. Of course, once you have accepted the fact that your own energy is the (unlimited) supply of all your stuff and life circumstances, it hardly makes sense to spend that energy on people or situations that are less than worthy of your greatness. But, if you haven't done it already, spend some time getting clear on your goals, doing whatever work you need to do to make sure you're not still focused on beliefs like "I only need enough money to get by," or "I don't deserve success," and then setting your goals and thoughts on positive things so that the right blueprints of your life are being delivered.

So, now that we've talked about forming your mental "pictures" for the stuff you want in your life, we'll move on to how to keep the most energy moving toward those pictures. Remember: no energy flow, no stuff!

7

Build, Don't Spend!

My main goal with this book is to make you aware of
your energy and to establish a plan for helping you start
building that up, so if that's already happening, then
great! I did want to mention, though—in my experience,
even when you have your "supply" going, it is pretty
easy to "spend" that energy on habits you already have,
and this might end up creating things that you don't
necessarily want.

Of course, once you think about the fact that you're
actually "spending" your energy supply (which could
have been forming itself into your goals and money) on
people or situations you don't want, that might be
enough to make you stop. But, in case it's not, I thought
I'd give you some books/resources that have helped me
keep more of my own energy supply. If they don't work
for you, then just leave them behind. No judgment.

Once you've found your connection to your energy and have directed it toward forming your goals, you don't want anything holding you back! Here are some common things that might be "spending" your energy supply, including limiting beliefs, bad habits, or an affinity for drama. Change just one of these things, and you could redirect a flood of energy into your life.

If you've been working on personal development for awhile, you may have already heard of some of these concepts. However, when you combine them in this way and bring in this new level of understanding of your own energy supply, things will start to change. Once you realize, hey, my energy literally **becomes** money, you might get a little more motivated to not only stop giving your energy away, but to think of ways to stay connected to it, and even to build it up. Here are some common challenges that I've had and that people I know have dealt with. If you'd like to suggest some more (as well as some methods or resources of overcoming them), I'm all ears!

Challenge # 1: A Wandering Mind, and an Inability to Stay in the Moment

Why, you might ask, even when you have all this new information about how the world works, plus instructions on how to build up your energy, is it still so difficult to get your thinking mind to stop racing around, thinking of new ideas and ways to "make" things happens? Doesn't it understand that the actually the opposite is true and that the best plan is for it to spend more time focusing on the flow of energy, more time "allowing" energy and prosperity, and less time wearing itself out?

No, it does not understand.   It's hard to get your thinking mind to give it a rest, and the reason for that is: habit. Even when your mind starts to accept the truths about energy, it still needs to be re-trained, because it still goes into the same patterns and habits it always had. This is human nature, of course. We don't always do what's best for ourselves, even if we know it's good for us. Ever try to start an exercise program? They say the hardest part is actually getting your shoes and gear on and going down to the gym. This is even more difficult when it's your mind we're talking about, because your mind (ego) is going to keep saying things like "I don't have time for this!" or "I'm too busy!" or "Thinking and planning and obsessing has gotten me this far!" or "Building up energy is a waste of time" or maybe "I have to check my email." If you're like 99% of everyone who tries to start a new habit, you're going to encounter some resistance on the road to meditation. That's why daily consistency and commitment are so important, especially at the beginning. So, for the purposes of our "energy experiment" here, it would be great if you could put your skepticism on hold and start to accept that your own energy is the basis for your life, and set about on a meditation program to connect with and build up that energy. This will make it a whole lot easier to have a constant "flow" going.

At first, this will seem totally weird, and it really will feel like you can either do one or the other. Either you're meditating, or you're engaging your conscious mind to do practical things. However, as your meditation practice becomes more and more a part of your life, you will find that it's easier to feel your own energy (or life force) while you're doing practical things, so it doesn't have to be one or the other. This is a good thing to practice, because (like the other energy exercises in this book), it has the end result of making your life go more smoothly, and building up the energy from which your life is formed. Hey, you couldn't always talk on the phone and check Facebook at the same time, right? If you can "multitask" in other areas of your life, there is no reason why you can't add "keep flow of energy going" to your list (although, in truth, the more you do this one thing, the less you have to do the others). The result is a steady stream of energy and "flow" in your life.

Things to try: The work of Eckhart Tolle might really help you stay "in the present moment." Remember, that "presence" is your energy! Also, try going back to some of the methods in the chapter on "Energy Building Activities." It's just a matter of building up the habit. You will get the hang of it!

If you are open to more "alternative" techniques, the Emotional Freedom Technique (EFT) is an interesting and effective form of "tapping" (a sort of self-acupressure) of energy points to help release blocks. Carol Look is an amazing EFT expert and is very helpful in getting to the root of what might be holding you back. Visit her site at www.attractingabundance.com for more information and programs that can help.

Challenge # 2: Resistance

Listen, no one is saying you have to love everyone and everything—that would be inauthentic. But, if it's possible, you might want to start inclining your mind toward "emotional mastery." Here's why: if you get caught up in something you just can't let go of, you're spending your energy supply. If you dwell on "drama" or negative situations, you're spending your energy supply. You don't need to love everything if that doesn't feel natural, but you *do* need to train your mind to be relaxed and to allow the flow of energy to be constant. You really have to form habits that will keep the portals open!

While you're still getting used to the concept of energy and developing the habit of building it up in your life, try not to distract yourself with things like fighting, judgment, or whatever you know drains your energy supply. Only you know what this is for you. This, really, is what is meant by "accepting what is"—you must stop fighting against what seems like adversity in your life, and turn back and reconnect with your own energy so that you can get what you want. Do the thing you have to do or interact with the "difficult" person if you must, but bring to this interaction whatever (small) level of engagement that allows you to stay connected with your own energy. That is to say, if arguing with someone causes you to forget your connection and go totally unconscious, where you are no longer aware of your energy, then you will need to train yourself to stop doing that. Do not let circumstances pull you out of this consciousness and back into your regular thoughts and routine. This will "unplug" the flow of energy, and no one wants that.

Use whatever method works for you—it is very important that you achieve an uninterrupted awareness of your own energy, and only you know what is going to be important to helping you do that. Consider this—when you *spend* your time and energy resisting, judging, or fighting against a situation, you are literally *spending* your energy—that thing that we've established turns into money when you visualize money. This means that you're actually **paying** to extend a bad situation. Yikes! Save your energy for yourself and your new life. Engage in a less than optimal situation only as much as you have to, and make sure that you're giving most of your focus to staying connected to the energy within you. The quickest way to make a situation resolve is to set the goal for what you'd like the resolution to be (for instance, "a new job/living situation"), then focus back in on strengthening that connection and building your inner storehouse of energy. By doing this, you are essentially building that new situation with your own energy, and it's going to happen a lot faster if you're not building it up, then spending it down again by paying attention to the crappy situation. Ignore, if you have to. Just don't engage.

Challenge # 3: I Can't Stop Thinking Negative Thoughts

If you are a person who dwells on the past, re-hashes old events to death and can't let go, or constantly dwells on stress and negative outcomes, you can be sure that these habits/thought patterns are costing you, since they are causing you to "spend" your energy. Yes, it is hard to put old situations and hurts behind you and to accept less than ideal circumstances, but now you have a tangible reason to do these things— if your energy becomes your money and success, then you want to keep as much of it as you can, and you especially don't want to be spending it on people or circumstances who have caused you harm.

Believe me, I totally sympathize with this one—I was raised in a completely pessimistic family. My grandparents survived the Depression, and they thought everything was a bad idea. They didn't want anyone spending money, taking risk, or even having big dreams. They weren't terribly happy themselves, and they made everyone around them afraid to start anything for fear that the sky would fall, or that you'd lose everything and have to sleep in a box. Actually, they never said "sleep in a box," but I guessed that this was what they were thinking. It's taken me years of hard work and "feeling the fear and doing it anyway" to get their voices out of my head, but this has gotten a lot easier once I realized that negative thoughts *spend* energy, and positive ones *build* it. When you think about it, this means that my grandparents' philosophies and constant negative thoughts probably cost them millions over the years!

Think of it this way— if your energy can be directed to become your money, then every time you re-hash a negative event, or tell someone about how much you hate your boss, or dwell on how your dad abandoned your family, you are essentially spending your energy supply on stuff you don't want. These "energy residuals" are the best reason to do what you need to do in order to get past that situation, whether it's in therapy, writing in a journal, or simply telling your mind once and for all that this situation is over and that you're not willing to give it any more of your energy (money, goals, etc.). Books like Louise Hay's "You Can Heal Your Life" and Byron Katie's "Loving What Is" can help you let go and move on. The Sedona Method is also really good for this, and that is why after learning their methods of "releasing," you will be able to (according to the Sedona Method website) "eliminate suffering and create all your heart's deepest and most worthy desires." By releasing stuff that you're dwelling on, you will be able to build up energy that much faster, which will then appear as your goals. Simple!

Let It Go

If you're finding this concept overwhelming, just commit to trying it for a week. Set your goals, work on building your energy, and try not engaging in drama or painful memories, just for a week. If you see things beginning to take shape in a positive way, you'll know you've found your "leak," and you're on the right track to the life you've always dreamed of. A year from now, you will thank yourself when your grudge against someone (who's probably stuck in the same place in their life) is a distant memory and you are fantastically successful! As they say, living well is the best revenge. Not that you're thinking about revenge; you're thinking about your own supply of energy, and that is enough.

All this is not to say that you can never see hurtful people or think about these situations again. Of course, that would be denial, and these feelings have to go somewhere. Just make sure you figure out a way to come to a point of enough acceptance so that you don't get caught up again and start spending your energy. No energy residuals!

Clear out the garbage and limiting thoughts that might be holding you back. Honestly, a consistent practice of meditation/energy building is going to really help with these, as it will make you feel more confident and powerful, but please take whatever steps necessary to rid yourself of useless things like thinking, "I'm a loser" or "I will always be poor because my parents said so."

Why would you want to do all that work building up your energy, only to have it make negative situations happen? Set your goals (in the positive, of course), focus on your energy, and leave it at that. If you need help overcoming a negative self-image, by all means pursue whatever help feels right to you. If you're stuck and can't "clear out" this negative stuff, go over to Carol Look's site at http://attractingabundance.com and EFT a try. You might be surprised at the results!

Challenge # 4: I Can't Get "Happy" for Something I Don't Have Yet

Usually in law of attraction studies, emotions are broken down into two categories—good emotions, which are said to be getting you closer to what you are wanting, and "bad" emotions like fear and anger, which are getting you further away. There is also mention of "vibrational harmony"— that is, trying to get yourself to feel the feeling you'll have when you get what you want.

But, what if it's even simpler than that? What if the difference between the two sets of emotions is that the "good" ones build your energy, while the "bad" ones deplete it, thus providing a perfectly logical (and quantifiable) explanation for why feeling good gets you there?

As we've discussed, the "good emotions" that you're feeling (and they're unique to everyone—no one but you knows what makes you feel good) are actually producing and multiplying your own energy, which is then used to actually form your goals and intentions.

Again, this is creation, not attraction. You are building up the energy that ultimately becomes what you want, like a car or a house. Or, rather, by connecting with the energy within you, you are allowing that energy to build up, eventually forming what you're intending.

The bottom line: put yourself in a happy and joyful state (however you get there), and you will build more energy, thereby getting (creating) what you want that much more quickly. Feel the "bad" emotions, and you'll make bad stuff or nothing at all.

Does this mean you should start forcing yourself to feel happy for no reason, for something you don't have yet, just to build up more energy?

Well—yes, and no. If you're one of the lucky people who can call up genuine positive emotions at will, then fantastic! It will probably work. In fact, if you are in the habit of being in a very naturally happy person, you have probably already noticed that your goals (when you set them) tend to have a lot of energy behind them, and that things fall into place for you. Luckily, you are able to connect with your own energy, and are serving as your own renewable energy source, just from your attitude. Assuming that you don't have any energy-sapping habits like yelling at talk radio, you probably just need to set some goals and take some action, and you'll be on your way. Maybe just realizing this will make you so happy you'll set a goal for making a million dollars, or ending hunger in Africa, and away you'll go!

There's been an enormous amount of talk within the study of the law of attraction about emotions— good emotions, bad emotions, using your emotions to get into "vibrational harmony" with what you're trying to attract, feeling the emotions associated with already having the thing you desire, and so on.

For most people (me included), this is the "sticking point" of the manifestation process, as you can never really convince your thinking mind to feel truly happy about something it knows it clearly doesn't have yet. You can pretend, feel happy about something you have and then transfer the feelings, or however you get there, but honestly, this is one of the most problematic things about "The Secret," and the thing that experts seem to go back to time and again, claiming that you didn't get what you wanted because you were out of vibrational harmony, or you obviously didn't really feel the emotions of having the thing strongly enough to bring it in.

To this, I will say the same thing you're probably saying: What?? That sounds crazy.

Here are the facts: to get stuff, you need energy. To get energy, you need connection. For *some* people, having happy emotions about the goal itself makes the connection and builds the energy. And look, if you're one of the people who can get yourself in the good-feeling zone by really feeling what it will be like when you have achieved the object of your desire, then great! Do that. You obviously have great access to your emotions, and are able to use them as a tool to build your energy.

Here's the thing. You don't need to feel the emotion of having *that* experience in order to "bring it in" or "attract" it. In fact, that is not even really what's happening— you just happen to be building up energy in conjunction with that visualization, if it makes you feel happy when you think about it.

If you can't do this, though, you can still get what you want, just by feeling that "aliveness" however you feel it and taking consistent action toward your goal. Energy is actually a pretty arbitrary thing, kind of like water-- once you have a lot of it built up (through meditation, good emotions, or whatever other method you've found that works), it will go where you direct it. One method that is taught very frequently in law of attraction studies is to visualize, and really get into the feeling where you have what you are wanting. If this is working for you, then it's another effective method of generating energy toward your goal, nothing more. You don't even have to get too attached to not being able to feeling that emotion for that specific thing.

If your thinking mind/ego can't really get past the fact that you *don't* have these things yet, then this is simply a method that doesn't generate energy for you, period. You don't need to "clear the blocks," or visualize a different way, or take a personal coaching program to teach you how to achieve "vibrational harmony." This is what works for these particular people, but if it doesn't work for you, worrying over how you're not doing it right or obsessing over different methods is only going to spend your energy. Our goal here is to find that energy *within you* and grow it, right?

If you don't happen to be the kind of person who feels comfortable feeling happy for a car you don't have yet (and believe me, I'm right there with you), don't worry about it. That method does help some people access their own energy, but is not the only way.

Want proof? Here's an example: Alec Baldwin experienced a phenomenal career resurgence in the 2000s. His *30 Rock* role won him numerous Emmys, he's starring in commercials, he just got married and had a new baby, and he's doing the best work of his life. However, a recent New Yorker profile clearly shows that Baldwin doesn't spend any time whatsoever "in gratitude," or "feeling the satisfaction of achievements," whether he's achieved them or not. In fact, Alec

Baldwin has what everyone can probably agree is a terrible attitude, and according to law of attraction experts, this should mean that his life is a shambles.

Not so! Baldwin has a source of energy that we don't know about. Maybe it's sailing his boat around the harbor (the one thing he actually claims to enjoy during the interview). Maybe he meditates. Maybe once he got onto the set of *30 Rock*, he felt happy, and this built his energy up. All I'm saying is, he's clearly not getting there through positive emotions, so if you can't mold your feelings to fit the future, there is still hope for you. Energy is energy! Find the way to connect to yours!

Just set your goal and do your meditation, or go surfing, or do anything that generates a good feeling for you. It's not so much (or at all) what the good feeling is caused by, just that you're feeling the connection and generating the energy.

Remember: it's *your* energy! Build, don't spend!

8

Fine Tuning

Wellness is a condition involving every aspect of your being—body, mind, and spirit...To be truly well means to be operating in a constant dance of pushing past previous limits and breaking new ground.

Kathy Freston, "Quantum Wellness"

This chapter is primarily about nutrition, since some nutritional choices (or lack thereof) can put a "kink in the hose" of some people's energy. I really want to emphasize here—no one is trying to tell you what to do, and I'm not saying that these things work for everyone, just that some of them have worked for me or for other people whom I've observed to be very successful. If you feel fine and healthy and have already started seeing big changes in your life, feel free to skip it!

1. Cut Vegetarian/Go Organic

Unless you live in a totally rural area, chances are you have access to a Whole Foods, Trader Joe's, or other healthy-type food store, so if this option appeals to you, go there and get some meat and dairy alternatives! Try beans, tofu, or veggie burgers for a month, and if you feel super-human and like you're suddenly able to really feel your energy, then more power to you (literally!). On the other hand, if doing without meat makes you weak and anemic (which it does for some people), do yourself a favor and at least switch over to organic and/or free range meat products. It's better for the planet, plus you don't want cruelty, hormones, and chemicals weighing you down. Plus, Kathy Freston (of "Quantum Wellness" fame) says her life took a quantum leap forward when she eliminated animal products. Her book was featured by Oprah and was a *New York Times* bestseller, in case you're wondering about her ability to channel that energy into success. Alicia Silverstone is a longtime vegan who swears by the health and spiritual attributes of an animal-free diet, and Paul McCartney has long extolled the virtues of a meat-free existence. Other famous and successful vegetarians include Chris Martin from Coldplay, Madonna, Pamela Anderson, Russell

Simmons, and many, many more. Visit www.peta.org for a free "Get Started With Vegetarianism" kit, or go to www.kathyfreston.com.

2. Give Up Caffeine

Those who believe in a caffeine-free life claim that this stimulant does everything from inhibiting sleep to causing mental illness. This might be true of anything in high enough quantities, but for some people, giving up caffeine makes their brain work better. It could be true that all the coffee and soda you've been drinking is making your mind race and is clouding your thoughts, which in turn is making it tough for you to meditate and to focus on what you want. Some people even say that consuming caffeine makes them more likely to think negative thoughts.

Maybe you've been drinking caffeine since college, and you don't even know what you'd be like without it. Some people find that they feel much more spiritually "awake" when they remove caffeine from their systems—maybe this is you! If you suspect that being over-caffeinated is blocking your ability to get what you want, try eliminating caffeine in all its different forms (including coffee, soda, and chocolate) for a month and see how you do. A great book to help you taper off (and to help you learn more about the effects of caffeine) is "Caffeine Blues," by Stephan Cherniske. Cherniske is a passionate anti-caffeine advocate, his theories are interesting, and he offers an "off the bean" program for getting yourself off of caffeine without the dreaded headaches. Chermiske's simple test for finding out if caffeine is adversely affecting your nervous system? Put your hand out in front of you. If it's shaking, even a little bit, you're drinking too much. Think of what that's doing to your brain! I personally had a hard time with this one because I could not find a decent substitute and I missed the ritual of having a hot drink in the morning (I don't like tea). Finally I found Dandy Blend, which tastes enough like coffee to satisfy the urge, which also giving you the health benefits of dandelions! I know, it sounds weird, but try it! www.dandyblend.com for more information.

3. Stamp Out Cigarettes

You've heard how bad smoking is for you, and you're probably planning on quitting anyway, so why not now? Cigarettes constrict the blood flow to your brain, which is basically the key element involved in your awareness of your personal energy. Think of it this way—the more you smoke, the less energy you are able to realize, and the less money you will earn (or success you will have, or less dream house, or whatever your thing is). Remember, you are forming those things out of your own energy, so anything that limits or stops the flow (including negative associations and guilt about smoking and the nagging sense that you're slowly killing yourself) is really holding you back. Many people have reported huge leaps forward in their ability to build up and direct their energy once they give up this nasty habit. But again, don't take my word for it. Give it 60 days (to get the nicotine out of your system, and see for yourself how good you feel. Visit www.smokefree.gov

4. Drink More Water

Water: A huge percentage of us don't get enough of it, and a dehydrated body and brain are only going to bring you down. Signs of chronic dehydration include fatigue, weight gain, acne, constipation, confused thinking, and joint pain. Adding more water into your diet is one of the easiest ways to get yourself back on the road to good health and a breakthrough in your energy.

A great book to read on this subject is "Water: for Health, for Healing, for Life," by Dr. Fereydoon "Batman" Batmanghelidj. Dr."Batman" spent over twenty years researching the miraculous effects of proper hydration, and his many books on the subject claim that simply upping your water intake will address many medical ailments, help you lose weight and make your brain work better. Visit www.watercure.com , or just pick up a glass of water!

5. Take Fish Oil

If you are eating the standard American diet (and no judgments, most of us are), you are probably deficient in Essential Fatty Acids. EFAs help your brain work better (as well as making your skin look great and lubricating your joints). Obviously, if you're able to make your brain function better (indeed, in some cases, enough fish oil has been shown to help depression, anxiety, and ADD), you will be able to more easily point your thoughts toward what you want, and expand your consciousness in a positive direction, which might lead to a breakthrough in and of itself. Again, it can't hurt to try, because you're probably deficient anyway. Be sure to get high-quality (pharmaceutical grade) fish oil. Dr.

Barry Sears has a great book on this subject, called "The Omega RX Zone," which includes recommendations of brands to try. Dr. Daniel Amen (author of the bestseller "Change Your Brain, Change Your Life") advocates getting the proper amount of EFAs. Visit www.amenclinic.com or www.zonediet.com, and be sure to ask your doctor if you have questions about adding fish oil to your diet, as it might conflict with medications or certain health conditions.

6. Get Some Exercise

There are a thousand guides and methods out there, and seemingly every day someone introduces a new method of exercise that is the "magic cure all." Your mission (should you choose to accept it) is to find a form of exercise that you can do at least five days a week. I really like walking outside, and have expanded this habit to include up to two hours per day, six or seven days a week. Exercise helps you connect and build your inner supply of energy. It makes you feel good, and it keeps you healthy. If you're not doing some form of regular exercise now, please—put on your shoes and go for a walk, or get in the pool, or whatever strikes your fancy. Just make sure it's something you like enough to be able to do it at least thirty minutes per day. You don't need a complicated set of weights or a gym to put on a pair of shoes and take a walk, or to dust off your bike, put on your helmet, and get out there. Exercise is important to your overall success and mental health (and consequently, your buildup of energy). Exercise will help you live longer, blow the cobwebs out of your brain, get you physically stronger to meet the challenges of life, and hopefully make it so you can also wear smaller pants. Only you know what type of exercise (or diet, or meditation) is going to be the best for you and is going to work best with your schedule, but please include it on your list of "most important things to do" if you don't have a regular routine at this time. Here are some resources to get you started with exercise:

1. Tony Robbins' "Get the Edge" program—
   excellent for helping you clean up all areas of
   your life, and includes an audio program to get
   you out and walking right away. Order it on
   www.tonyrobbins.com, borrow it from a friend,
   or get it on eBay. This program is totally worth
   the money if you don't know where to start.
   Laugh if you will, but Tony Robbins is very

motivational!

2. Here is a list of ten popular sports/forms of
   exercise. Look over it and take notice of anything
   that jumps out at you.

   - Running/walking
   - Swimming
   - Biking
   - Tennis
   - Soccer
   - Surfing
   - Going to the gym/taking exercise classes
   - Dancing
   - Pilates
   - Yoga

Right now, figure out which one of these you're going to
start, and commit to doing it a couple of times a week
for a month Your goal should be to work up to doing
some kind of exercise or physical activity every day, just
to keep healthy and fit and keep your energy moving.
One of my friends recently joined "Curves" because she
was really bothered by an extra ten pounds and the

constant thinking about it. After she started going regularly, she sold her house for a profit (during the recession) and got a new job. Coincidence? Maybe. Maybe she just really loves *Curves*.

7. Cut Out Alcohol, or Drugs, or Both

Like I said in the beginning of this chapter, no one is trying to tell you what to do—this is all about getting you connected to your own energy supply, and/or cutting out impediments that might be "blocking the channel" for that energy, so to speak. So, if you drink a lot or take drugs, maybe so much that you feel guilty about it or it takes up a lot of your time or causes you to feel "unconscious" or like you're really disconnected from the flow of life, maybe cut down and see if you notice some changes. Just from a nutritional standpoint, alcohol and drugs can affect the way your brain works, which can affect your ability to be aware of your own energy supply. But again, only you know if this is an issue for you. We can certainly all name some super-successful people who drink and/or use drugs, and this doesn't seem to affect their energy supply at all.

8. Cut Out Sugar.

I'm sure you've heard that scary statistic about how Americans eat 150 - 170 pounds of sugar per year. If this is you, and your sugar habit has caused some unwanted weight gain, and you spend a lot of time thinking "I'm so fat" and beating yourself up about your eating habits, and are continually making plans about how you have to start exercising... I'm sure you can see where I'm going with this. If this happens to be an issue for you, you might be spending a lot of your energy on these thoughts, which is just making more of what you don't want. Breaking the sugar habit is a good place to start, since sugar is corrosive to your system and your brain anyway, and you'll probably save a lot of money and feel much better by just cutting it out. Think of it this way— if you cut out junk food, and by doing so you lose weight, and this frees up your energy to make your life even better, then essentially you're getting paid to be healthy. Awesome!

9. Cut Out Aspartame and Other Artificial Sweeteners.

I'm not saying Diet Coke is keeping you from being successful or wealthy, but if you're having headaches, gastrointestinal symptoms, blood sugar issues, or memory problems, or you're not able to lose weight, and you happen to drink a lot of Diet Coke, you might want to think about eliminating artificial sweeteners from your diet. Bottom line—these substances can make you feel crappy, which can interfere with your ability to get (and stay) in the flow. If you're interested in the (many) physical maladies that can be caused by overdoing it on the aspartame, visit www.sweetpoison.com.

10. Go On a Fast or Cleanse

Maybe you're finding this list a little overwhelming, and are one of those people who likes to get things done all at once. You might benefit from a short fast or cleanse to get some gunk out of your system. If it makes you feel just a little bit better or kick-starts you out of a bad habit (like eating too much chocolate), then it will more than likely let in some energy. Remember, any energy that's not being tied up in other places is being used to make your goals! There is a ton of information online about the "Master Cleanse," which is basically cayenne pepper, maple syrup, and lemon juice. Visit www.themastercleanse.org for more information. Personally, I have never been on this one because it seems a little too hard-core for me, but I have used the "Arise and Shine" products with success, which you can find at www.ariseandshine.com.

If you already do (or don't do) some of the things on this list, great! If not, try adding (or subtracting) them one month at a time, and be sure to keep a journal so you can see what's working. Something is going to make the energy difference for you!

9

Desperate Times, Desperate Measures

We've all been there—you get laid off from your job, get behind on your mortgage or credit cards, or suddenly find yourself alone. This is the time when most people are moved to action, the time when most people's "thinking mind" takes over and starts making plan after plan, one of which is sure to "turn things around." Not unlike a drug addict, we grow more and more desperate for a response or result from the outside world.

Ironically, the more we act, the less seems to happen. The more times we call a person, the less they want to talk to us. The more resumes we send out, the fewer interviews we get. The more we become fixated on new ways and ideas to get money, the more quickly our funds dry up.

But, why? Why should it be the case that the harder you push something (or someone), the more it resists you? Why is it that the best time to get a job is when you already have a job? The answer to these questions, of course, is energy supply. When your thinking mind becomes fixated and comes up with solution after solution ("Just call once more! Just send out one more headshot! All I need is a backer and my business will take off!"), you are unplugged from universal energy and are running on battery power. Like a cellphone that needs its charger, soon you will find that you're in the "dead zone," where your feverish desperation has taken over—you can't stop thinking about "when is this situation going to resolve," and yet by repeatedly thinking that, you have disconnected yourself from your own life force, insuring that it won't (or that it will take longer).

Here's an example of this phenomenon: women who struggle with infertility often take years to become pregnant with their first child. Once they finally achieve their goal of motherhood (either through extensive fertility procedures, adoption, surrogacy, or other means), they unexpectedly find themselves pregnant for a second time with no effort at all (or for the first time if their first child came to them through adoption). The missing element in this situation is energy —they were so focused on that desperate longing for a child that they spent all of their energy in that direction. Once they stopped focusing their time (and energy) on that first pregnancy, their energy supply began to build up again. This results in the goal (a child) being fulfilled, sometimes several times over. The key is the re-focusing of the mind to allow the energy to begin to build up.

So, what if you're in one of these desperate (de-spirited) mindsets? The solution is to re-connect and re-focus your mind on your own life energy. Use whatever means you can to keep your "thinking mind" or ego from running amok looking for solutions. Meditate more frequently, listen to music, and laugh. Play with your dog.

In case you're wondering—yes, it does seem counter-intuitive to be playing with your dog or taking a walk on the beach when the world seems to be falling down around you. But, here's the thing—your focusing on the bad situation is only making it worse. By taking some time out to feel good, you will interrupt the negative cycle and start to allow some energy to flow into the solution again. The more you do this, the faster the situation will resolve. While the "thinking mind" may try to label this as escapism or denial, the truth is that once you've done everything you can and have your intention in mind, there is nothing more you can do, and you need to let it go and allow your energy to flow into the situation. No one is disputing the fact that serious things happen in life—times get tough, and it is perfectly normal for your mind to want to solve the whole situation. The real solution is for you to take as much action as feels "inspired," then when you feel like you're pushing it or nothing's happening, to immediately pull back and re-connect with your energy.

Do What You Can Do, Then Leave It!

One of the hardest things when you're going through a hard time is knowing when to say when. It really does seem like the more hours you work on something, the more results you'll get. Simple equation, right?

Unfortunately, when it comes to your supply of energy, the answer is no. In fact, when you are facing a challenging situation, there will come a time (and you will be able to feel it) when you are "beating a dead horse," so to speak. No one is calling you back, the emails have stopped coming, and you have zero prospects in your work or money situation (or whatever you're trying to resolve). Maybe you're on your 100th negative pregnancy test, or you've sent out 1,000 resumes. Maybe you've used the last of your money to pay a bill, and you don't know what to do from there. Back in the day, we used to call this phenomenon "having leprosy." No offense to people with actual leprosy, but you see what I mean. Some days, it feels like you just can't win.

Right then is the time to say "enough is enough." Your thinking mind (ego) has tried to solve the problem through sheer dedication and will, and was not successful in resolving the situation. There is nothing more it can do, and you must give it a new assignment: focusing on the energy inside yourself. Focus and connect, and build that energy back up!

Therefore, from now on, when you are facing a situation that you really need to resolve, you are going to do the following:

1. Set It and Forget It

Yes, it's an old cliché, but it really applies to this situation. Give yourself a task list (like "send five resumes" or "call five people" or "send five query letters to agents/newspapers"), then go right back to your preferred method of connecting with your inner energy and building it up. As of now, your thinking mind/ego has been reassigned. It has one set of tasks per day, which it will gladly accomplish. When you feel it starting to get crazy and desperate, you will immediately know it is time to shift your focus back to the energy within you, because once you've completed those tasks, you are "pushing it," and as we've discussed, pushing it this eats up the very energy that is trying to turn into your goal. Yes, it's that simple. Do your tasks, then take your attention **away** from pursuit of the goal. This will allow your energy a chance to build up.

2. Get Your Emotions Under Control

What if you're dealing with chaotic and seemingly uncontrollable negative emotions like anger, or judgment, or resentment? Self-help experts will tell you to "let feelings go" because they cause illness, make it difficult to achieve your goals, and make it hard for you to relate to other people. That's fine, but what if you still feel angry? It's hard to let go of the past, right? It's hard to stop judging, to "live and let live," and to not let those stupid politicians and noisy neighbors and bad drivers and loud cellphone talkers eat you up inside. How can you let your anger go when the world is falling apart? There's bad news all around you, and you'd be crazy not to feel it, right? There is a certain amount of justifiable anger that goes along with being human, right? If we just passively accept all situations, then aren't we just asking for more of same?

All good points. But, what if you got paid to figure out a way to ignore things that cause you to feel negative emotions (the ones that drain you of energy)? What if you got money when you turned off the news or trained yourself to redirect that rage you feel when someone cuts you off in traffic or your in-laws are being unreasonable?

Maybe you can see where this is going. If you're focusing attention (and you can tell you're doing this if you're feeling negative emotions on a regular basis) on whatever gets you riled up, you are literally spending energy that, when otherwise directed, could be turned into money or beneficial circumstances in your life. That is to say, if you have a goal to be a multi-millionaire, you are going to get there a lot faster if you build your energy (which we've already established) will be translated into your life as money or things), and don't waste any of it resenting, being angry, or judging. It's really just a thing you're doing for yourself: if energy turns into money, then why would you want to give some of yours to a guy who is pissing you off by playing his stereo too loud? You'd be much better off setting the intention for peace and quiet, then doing what you can to re-connect and get the flow going again, whether that's by going for a walk, playing with your dog, or calling a friend to go out to a movie. Frankly, you don't even have to "accept" the obnoxious people or circumstances. "Acceptance," in this sense, just means finding a way to allow it enough that you're not paying it your attention. Get it? Don't *pay your attention* (energy) toward situations that you don't want, and they won't come back. Pay your attention toward what you don't want, and you are actually contributing to the loud stereo, or the bad driver, or the nasty boss. Just re-connect with your own energy, and focus on your outcome. No one is saying you have to like or want more of what's going on, but it will resolve much faster if you pay your attention elsewhere.

Remember—your energy is your money! Save yours for yourself and the world, and don't spend it on obnoxious things.

But, what is it about a crappy situation that just takes over your mind? When you're in one, it's all you notice, all you think about, and it seems to last forever. Why? How is that even useful? And how are you supposed to get yourself out of it when it's everywhere you turn? We've all been there, and the answer to "How do I get out of it?," of course, is to try to relax, set the goal /intention of what you want (like more money, or a healthy body, or a new living situation), then put all of your effort toward connecting with your own energy, building that up, and letting the solution arise from there.

It's good in theory, but it sounds hard at the same time, right? What if you still have to live in a place you hate, or go to a job that makes you so stressed you're having panic attacks? Crappy situations pull your attention away from your own energy, and can get you stuck in the metaphysical sand trap of life, a "Groundhog Day" of sorts where your life energy is being used only to keep you alive and to replicate the same experience over and over again.

It's hard to stop thinking about bad stuff. Drama attracts attention, and our thinking minds will struggle and wrestle against it, just to let the universe know "I don't approve of that," not realizing that the mere act of noticing and disapproving is using your energy to create "more of the same." To add to the difficulty of "turning the other cheek," as Marci Shimoff mentions in her excellent book "Happy for No Reason:" "Our brains are like Velcro for negativity and Teflon for positivity," meaning that negative experiences tend to stick with us (for learning and evolutionary purposes, like remembering not to touch a hot stove), while positive ones roll off our backs. With this kind of habit already established in our brains, it is even harder to just tell ourselves to "just think positive and everything will turn out fine." Frustrating!

The way out, of course, is in. Do what you can to get

your situation as tolerable as you can, set a goal that resolves it, and then focus on re-connecting and building up that energy so that the solution can appear that much faster. Some people might call this "acceptance," but this is a word that has just never worked for me, since acceptance implies some sort of approval. I've been using "allowing it" or "putting it in the neutral zone" with success—to me, these terms imply that I'm simply not giving that situation any more of my energy. If you can't stand your apartment, go sit in the park and build up your energy. Do what you can to shift your attention away from the problem at hand and back to your inner energy, and the situation will resolve that much more quickly.

Does it seem not only counter-intuitive, but rather impossible to shift your attention away from the problem at hand and back to your own life energy?

Yes, it does. And it takes a significant amount of self-discipline and focus to train yourself not to get pulled back down into an all-consuming situation. But, if you've tried everything else to solve the problem and nothing is working, even your thinking mind will agree that taking your attention off of it, even for a few hours, in order to let some energy go toward the solution, is not going to hurt, right? You might even feel better, and that might be all it takes to turn the tide of energy toward the solution. It might take your thinking mind /ego a long time to accept this fact, but obsessing about a situation almost never helps to resolve it.

The good news is, once you get the hang of it, focusing on building your own energy feels good. More energy means your problems start to take care of themselves, and life in general will become easier. So, do yourself a favor—set the goal, then take your attention off the crappy situation and go back to building the energy. You'll be glad that you did (both right then, and when the situation resolves).

One important note: you're not just trying to distract yourself from the problem or to kill time until it goes away—you are purposefully taking yourself mentally out of the situation so that your mind can stop chewing on it over and over, and so you can re-connect and start building up again, energy-wise. If you choose an activity that makes you just as unconscious (like watching TV or shopping), your energy (and the situation) are likely to be the exact same as when you left them.

So, again, no one is trying to tell you what to do— these are all just suggestions. If possible, please choose an activity that makes you feel truly connected to get you back on the right track. Feel your energy, have a good time, and focus on what you want, not the fact that you don't have it right now. You will get there!

Things to try: The Sedona Method, any of Byron Katie's books, Cognitive Behavior Therapy, or anything else that will help you take your attention off of the situation and let it go, at least for the moment.

10

God, Religion, and Church

By now, you might have guessed the "inner presence" or "energy within" that we've been talking about is, by some, known as God. This actually does mean that by turning your awareness toward the God spirit within you, you are attracting and multiplying the energy that will be directed by you to form money and prosperity.

Where does that leave religion? Should you still go to church? These are complicated issues for each individual and their families to deal with. I suspect that as more people turn within and begin to discover their own prosperity by being aware of the life force (God) within them, any religion that focuses on an external, punishing, jealous or mythical God will start to become a thing of the past.

Now that we're delving deep into a discussion of energy, think about this strange fact for a moment: organized religions are some of the richest organizations in the world. This includes, but is certainly not limited to, Scientology, Catholicism, and Mormonism.

A New Religion?

No one is saying that there is not a place for weekly gatherings of joy, music, and community. The Agape International Spiritual Center (http://www.agapelive.com) is a good example of this. You can find (or form) meditation groups in your area by visiting http://meditation.meetup.com/.

Speaking of gatherings, Napoleon Hill mentions the "Mastermind Group" as an essential component of success, reminding us that as part of a Mastermind Group of their own, Thomas Edison, Henry Ford, and Harvey Firestone (of the Firestone tire fortune) were each able to overcome limited education and knowledge to become the greatest and most successful men of their time. Clearly, there is a purpose for the gathering together of like minds, and that purpose is to multiply energy—not only of the group, but of the individual by association. This "group gathering" can be most commonly found in religious settings, like in a church or temple.

However, if going to church or belonging to a religion (because you have negative associations) separates you from being aware of the God spirit within you, then it is robbing you of your energy and therefore of your wealth and abundance. Fortunately, if you really love and feel empowered by your church and its community, your increased consciousness and awareness will only be an attribute, making you more able than ever to give more money to causes you deem worthy.

The real question is: does your religion help you connect with and build your own energy? Only you know the answer, and only you can decide if your current religious system is right for you.

Here's a litmus test—if going to church brings you closer to that "alive" feeling (thus building your energy) then fantastic. Go for it! Some of the most connected and successful people in the world cite their religions as a major force in their lives. Religion helps you connect with yourself, your community, and gives you a chance to really focus on your inner life, at least once a week. The question is—*does it feel right to you?*

Of course, religion is a very personal choice, and no one is trying to tell you what to believe, but since we all want to be as powerful and "in the flow" as possible, let's all try to choose whatever belief system that empowers us and brings out our inner sense of aliveness (which we now acknowledge is the energy that our stuff is made of). God wants you to be prosperous of course, because to the universal energy, "prosperous" means that you are connect and building it up. Of course, in your personal reality, a great deal of "God consciousness" or awareness of your own energy, or whatever you'd like to call it, might mean that you end up with a Rolls Royce, and that would also be very heavenly, if you know what I mean.

11

Questions and Answers About Energy

During the research and formation of this "energy philosophy," I was often asked questions that I thought were interesting ways to deepen the discussion. I have included some of them here.

Q: Isn't it selfish to use this breakthrough in consciousness as a means to get stuff? Shouldn't we be focused on getting in touch with our energy because it's the right thing to do for our fellow man, and because the consciousness of the human race must, as Eckhart Tolle says, "evolve or die?"

A: Not really. Since this is where our minds are focused, it is actually the most logical way in. Everyone comes to know their own energy and abilities at different stages and at different times in their lives. Wouldn't it be better for you if you could get yourself out of debt and get a new car, and be raising global consciousness at the same time? You'll be happy to know that by getting in touch with your energy and raising your level of consciousness, you'll be doing both.

Q: So...where do I start?

A: First, read through Chapter One and make the connection between "your energy" and the energy that is making up everything in your life. This new truth can actually take a long time to be fully accepted by your consciousness, so that is something to work on. Once you've accepted this truth, use any method you can find to connect to that ever-present energy, which is always flowing into your life (the existence of which is proven by your being alive). Meditation is the main component of this, as it literally connects you with the "higher power" energy that is keeping you alive (and making your stuff). The more you can be your own scientist, being in touch with that energy and start to really work with it through visualization, the more this will make sense.

Q: Why does it still take time to build up energy, even after I've made this acceptance part of my understanding?

A: Some spiritual teachers say that this shift—the shift of consciousness from the external to the internal— is one of the most difficult challenges of life, so in case you're not getting the hang of it right away, don't feel bad; you're in good company. The key thing to remember is that you're trying to change twenty-five (or thirty, fifty, or more) years of thinking something worked one way, and this is sometimes (okay, almost always) a very difficult thing for the reality-based thinking mind to accept. When you first try it, you'll be getting little bursts of energy here and there, which will be manifesting in unexpected money and improved circumstances (like coincidences and instant manifestations).

Rest assured—the more you think about and accept the fact that the energy /life force within you is the source of your experiences and material possessions, the more you'll "get it," and the more you'll see in your life. Once this idea is firmly accepted in your thinking and you are actively engaged in the practice of connecting to and building up that life energy, you will be surprised at how quickly things fall into place for you, and how the "evidence" will start to show up. For now, though, know that every time you make an effort to increase your consciousness (whether in the form of mediation, practicing feeling your "presence," listening to or reading personal development or spirituality books, or just enjoying yourself and listening to music), you are putting more of that energy in the "bank." With continued connection and growth, you will get what you want, no doubt about it. Your only job is to stay in the flow and build it up.

Q: Why would mankind be programmed with an automatic "blindness" for spiritual knowledge of this kind? Isn't the ego's resistance a sign that we should not be developing our connection to our own energy?

A: Absolutely not! The concepts of metaphysics and energy are more out in the open and part of the public conversation than ever before, so it is only a matter of time before the concept of building up your own energy becomes mainstream knowledge and we start to take it for granted, sort of like the way we now take for granted the fact that we have electricity in our homes, even though little more than a century ago, this was completely unheard of.

Look at it this way. It hasn't always been practical throughout the years for the "unwashed masses" to know that they had the kind of power we're talking about here. This is what is traditionally meant by "1% of the population makes 99% of the money." There has always been a certain portion of society that is familiar with these concepts and has used them to their fullest advantage. These individuals just know they are connected to something greater than themselves, a source of everything they want or need in life. Some describe this as a "silver thread to the universe;" some say it's just an unconscious knowing/belief.

To answer the question in historical terms, your ego's resistance is the result of thousands of years of conditioning by leaders (religious and otherwise) who wanted to keep people from getting too powerful and overthrowing them. You are re-conditioning your mind now, because these rules just don't apply to us anymore. Eventually your thinking mind/ego will get the hang of it, especially once it sees that focusing on and building energy yields much greater results than traditional hard work ever could.

Your mind will do what it's been trained to do (which is not necessarily what is best for you) until you point it in a different direction. If you come from a long line of smokers, drinkers, pessimists, or junk-food eaters, and you've changed this habit, you'll be familiar with the kind of mental work it took to change these ingrained habits, and know how much better you felt when you replaced these old habits and beliefs with newer, healthier ones.

When you accept the simple fact that it's your awareness of your own energy that is the single and most important factor in your success and fulfillment, it is easy to see how these things could never define you. Think of it this way: if it is true that all things come from energy, then it must also be true that what you can make from that energy is incidental and can't really define you, since you were the source all along. Therefore, you are not your car, or your job, or your house, or your circumstances... they are you, because what you are is the energy behind them. If you are unhappy with your circumstances and want things to be different, the solution is simply to focus in on, and thereby multiply, your energy, then direct it to a different place. If you are displeased with how that energy is currently being expressed in your life, simply point your attention in another (better) direction. Get it? You are in charge of the direction it goes! You do this by changing your thoughts and the things on which you are focusing. Focus on good things, and you'll make good things.

Q: By getting in touch with my own energy and directing that energy to form my prosperity, am I turning my back on God?

A: Absolutely not! You don't have to admit that there is no God—in fact, not even close. Clearly God *does* exist in the energy you feel within you, or else you'd be dead. You can even keep reading the Bible, if it is useful to you and helps you keep your life in order or makes you feel more connected to your own energy. But let's face it. The Bible as a manual for living is outdated. We as a society have seen things in our lifetimes that the writers (scribes) of the Bible could never even have dreamed of, and many of the rules outlined by the Bible were for the sole purpose of keeping society from falling apart and to keep people from getting hurt or hurting themselves or one another. So, don't let religion control you anymore. Find the God within yourself, develop your own relationship to this energy source, and then use it to create the life you want.

Q: If I'm feeling the life energy within me (what some people might call "God" or "the soul," using my conscious mind to gather it up (through meditation and awareness), and then I'm directing it (through visualization) to create the experience I want, doesn't that make me sort of God-like?

A: The answer is yes, and no, and yes. What you're doing is using your conscious mind (ego) to tap into your energy, then you're directing it. So, you could say you're tapping into God, or channeling God. Actually, you can call it whatever makes you feel most comfortable, as long as you're feeling connected and things are going smoothly for you. However, the minute your thinking mind/ego gets ahold of this concept, it's probably going to start shouting "I am God! I am God!" and break off on its own again, at which point you will have to double up on the meditation and awareness in order to re-connect with that energy within you and start to build it back up again. Your thinking mind is not God, but it really likes to think it is. The real God (energy) is within you, and is what you can feel when you quiet your thinking mind (ego). So, the more you can be aware of your energy, the more energy you'll have, plain and simple.

You will definitely find that the more of a rest you can give your thinking mind /ego and give that energy a chance to build up, the more "in the flow" your life will become. You will more easily achieve your goals, but you won't be as concerned about them because they won't define you. You will know that your only real purpose is to be in tune with that energy, and the positive side effect is that you'll have all the stuff you want. It's really the ultimate paradox, and you've probably always been aware of it. The more you want something, the less it happens. The less you want it, the more you get it!

Q: I've got my life in order and have started meditating regularly, and enjoy going to church. Is there room for religion in conjunction with the building and directing of energy?

A: Absolutely. If your life is running smoothly, you really feel your "aliveness," and you're able to set your goals and achieve them, then going to church or synagogue could really be your way to your own energy. Great! When you add a practice of daily meditation (the original and best way to build up energy), it will not only be a great addition to your life, but will push you up and over into a realm that you probably never imagined. Be sure to set some bigger goals!

Q: Okay, this seems pretty clear: your energy is the energy your stuff is made of. So, why don't more people talk about this?

A: Now is the first time in history in which our consciousness has been expanded enough to freely discuss energy and our connections to a universal life force. Our era is seeing the culmination of these ideas, and this is clearly indicated by the fact that we've never had a better understanding of the law of attraction, thanks to The Secret. Since we are now familiar with the ways to direct our energy to create the lives we've always wanted, all that is now missing is to is to connect one with the other, start to recognize that energy in ourselves, and build that energy in a purposeful way so that we might consciously use it to shape our experience.

The point of this book is to make that connection in your mind without using a specific religion or mentioning the word "God," as religious concepts are laden with so many thousands of years of beliefs and meanings, and tend to cloud the issue. Please, call the energy within you whatever you like. Just connect with it daily, experience it deeply during meditation, and feel it all the time in order to build it up.

Q: I have my life in order and have accepted the reality that my own energy is what's making my life, but don't really know if I've found my method of building up that energy. Nothing seems to really be happening, and my visualization feels "dead" and frustrated. Help!

A: First, go back to meditation, and work on finding a method that makes you feel connected with the energy that is inside you. A regular practice where you are really connecting with and building up your supply of energy is essential to build up the "bank account" of energy from which your life will be created. The more you practice a form of meditation that is right for you and really connects you to that life force, the more smoothly your life will start to go. You can probably stop a regular practice of visualization until you get the hang of meditation, since the visualization is unlikely to happen anyway without a good flow of energy, and because a constant undercurrent of frustration is bad for your state of mind, which (as we've said before) is depleting your energy.

If you haven't found your ideal meditation technique, don't give up! There are so many good methods out there (including the "sit quietly and feel your inner flow of energy" method), so you really should not stop in this pursuit until you've found something that you enjoy doing for at least twenty minutes, twice per day, just for the health and mental benefits that this practice will give you. The practice of meditation is arguably the most important part of your process of spiritual evolution on this earth, and it is your key to accessing the unlimited well of energy to get what you want in life. The more you do it, the easier it will become, and the more you'll find that you're actually living in that meditative, "connected" state, building energy all the time, only engaging your thinking mind/ego when you have to do something like pay bills or make plane reservations. If all of this seems too "over your head" or doesn't make sense right this minute, that's okay too. Just know that you're going to start connecting to your own energy, and that this is the key to getting what you want.

Also, ask yourself: "What do I love to do?" Is it surfing? Drawing? Walking on the beach? Listening to classical music? Each of us is unique, with a different access point into our own flow of energy. Maybe you need to find your way in from the outside, then remember that feeling and go back to it during meditation.

Q: Some literature on this subject says that I should "love everyone and everything." I work on this, but honestly don't feel these feelings toward my fellow man, or sometimes even myself. Should I keep trying?

A: I don't think so. You need to find what makes you feel alive and connects you with your own energy. For some, love is the emotion that makes them feel the most connected to their own energy, but it doesn't have to be love for specific things or people, and trying to live up to a universal "love everyone" standard is probably just going to make you feel bad (and drain your energy). Try to think of something (or someone) that you love, feel the energy associated with that, and go from there. Don't force yourself to do anything that feels artificial for you.

Q: What about "let go and let God?" Doesn't this mean I should just leave everything up to God or fate? This seems to be the opposite of what you're saying.

A: On the surface, this expression seems to mean that you should take your hands off the wheel of life and let God drive, so to speak.

This is great in theory, but there is definitely a step missing here. We can certainly "let go" of the thinking mind/ego's obsessive need to control everything, but we actually do need to "let God" flow in as the awareness of our own internal energy, which we will then direct toward real goals and circumstances in our lives. Far from being a passive activity that requires you to take your hands off the wheel, when you develop a consciousness of your own energy, your hands are firmly planted on the wheel of your destiny, because you are making the effort to stay in the moment and build the energy of your life. You (or, more accurately, your metaphysical energy) are the creator of your own destiny—not some arbitrary being in the ether. Your only job is to build your awareness of that energy so that it will appear in your life.

12

A New Connection, and a New Life

Since we've covered a great deal of information here, I'm going to close by saying that I hope that somewhere in this book, you had one of those "Aha!" moments that will help you connect with the energy within you so that your life will start to be "in the flow." It really is as simple as connecting to that energy within yourself, and every day, more people are coming into this new state of consciousness. This conversation is becoming more common every day!

Best of luck to you , and please share your stories by visiting any of the following:

www.wealthfromwithinbook.com
www.facebook.com/LoriCulwellAuthor
www.twitter.com/LoriCulwell

Free Bonuses

In case you didn't go over and get these bonuses at the beginning of the book, definitely do it now! Those free bonuses are yours and you should have them!

Visit this link:

http://wealthfromwithinbook.com/resources

to get the following books for free:

1. *Think and Grow Rich*, by Napoleon Hill

2. *The Master Key System*, by Charles Haanel

3. *Thoughts are Things*, by Prentice Mulford

4. *Our Invisible Supply: How to Obtain*, by Frances Larimer Warner

5. *The Science of Getting Rich*, by Wallace Wattles

6. *Your Invisible Power*, by Genevieve Behrend

Plus, a special audio bonus you can use for meditation!

Printed in Great Britain
by Amazon.co.uk, Ltd.,
Marston Gate.